SELF-INITIATION FOR SELF-RULERS

THE KING'S CURRICULUM

JOHNNY MANNAZ

The King's Curriculum
Self-Initiation for Self-Rulers

Johnny Mannaz
Copyright © 2020

Cover design by Srdjan Vidakovic
Book design by www.delaney-designs.com

ISBN Softcover: 978-1-7345713-0-1
ISBN Hardcover: 978-1-7345713-2-5
ISBN Ebook: 978-1-7345713-7-0

1.) Spirituality-Solar, 2.) Philosophy-Men, 3.) Self-Actualization (Psychology) 4.) Mythology- Psychological Aspects, 5.) Magic 6.) Occultism 7.) Thelema

LIVE YOUR WILL@www.thekingscurriculum.com

To my children:
Freyja Rosemond, Ursus Balder, and Ramsess Amun

…and to that Great Initiator
the Serpent in the Tree…

MANNAZ

LAPIS EXILIS

"He who is silent is forgotten,
He who does not advance,
Falls back.
He who stops is overwhelmed,
Distanced, crushed.
He who ceases to become greater,
Becomes smaller.
He who leaves off,
Gives up.
The stationary is the beginning of the end.
It precedes death.
To live is to achieve,
To WILL without ceasing."

Orison Swett Marden
An Iron Will

TABLE OF CONTENTS

THE CALL OF
SPIRITUAL KINGSHIP

"A Philosophy for the Few."

This is a book for those who hear "The Call" to claim their Crown and recognize their own "Divine Right": a life of Liberty and Sovereignty.

Answering this Call represents both the ultimate challenge and its attainment; it is both an opportunity and a choice, to fully "Live your Will."

Its premise is based upon that sublime realization that each individual is the rightful Sovereign of their consciousness. It acknowledges that the authentic nature of the Individual, their True Will, reflects the Will of the Universe. This implies that the authentic SELF is not only a Sovereign but an instrument of universal destiny.

Bestowed with this "Divine Right," is also the liberty granted the Individual to pursue the call of their own True Will and its fulfillment, thus attaining the ultimate completion of consciousness by forging a path to their own unique destiny.

Essential to embracing the rigors of this lifestyle is the stolid recognition that life, by its nature, is a battle: to be accepted, embraced, and faced with valor. From this noble perspective, it becomes clear how fortunate we are to be here, in this earthly life, where we are given the opportunity to "break a lance on that most ancient battlefield—of Free Will and Destiny."

It is through life's organic struggles—sacred competitions whose audience is the Gods—that individual glory is allowed to shine. Within a self-imposed chivalric code of honor, the Sovereign Individual is called to embrace all threats, obstacles, ordeals, impediments, and opponents as opportunities to exercise their Will and demonstrate its strength. In the same tradition, the Individual also willingly abolishes nihilism, regret, guilt, pity, sorrow, and despair.

The process of invoking the King's energy begins by fortifying one's mind and body for the challenges that occupation involves. Becoming a Master of one's own life means participating in a grand ritual of empowering *Oneself*, performing a series of sacred rites of becoming and enlisting all of nature's energies to add force and momentum to the task. This means constantly striving for higher goals and ideas. It means embracing the challenges of one's self-chosen occupation, making a daily practice of exceeding one's own perceived limits.

It is essential to do this unencumbered by the weight of the lowest common denominator, letting your true brilliance shine without concern for those who may fear your freedom or empowerment. When you "know thyself" and act accordingly, you are less likely than ever to "commit a wrong" in any higher sense.

Knowing your Will grants you the divine right—*to live it*. Ultimate liberty comes from becoming who you have the potential to be, ultimate success comes from cultivating your genius, and ultimate mastery comes from a mind-state that is harmonized with your True Will, and its Grand Vision.

Achieving this is the basis of self-mastery and facilitating this is the principal task of *The King's Curriculum*.

INTRODUCTION

B efore you lies a landscape of mystery, which is the terrain of your own subconscious mind. The Self-Initiation described in this book involves a journey into oneself and into a reality that forms the foundation of who you truly are at heart.

If you have ever wondered about the deepest aspects of your own nature, have questioned whether or not you were on an authentic path in life, or if you've been feeling a desire to understand your True Will more clearly, then you've picked up this book for a reason.

Nine challenges now lie before you, like lions guarding nine respective gateways of initiation, each building one upon another successively and yielding nine powers waiting to be unleashed as prizes for the victorious.

The challenges are straightforward and quite simple, in essence. Yet each possesses the potential to reveal qualities of hidden significance to the Initiate. You might imagine these challenges as portals of transformation, each acting as a distinct landmark on a journey of becoming. Each embodies a basic concept and utilizes a family of interrelated ideas to give structure to its underlying symbolism. Along with this, there is an image to capture the essence of each challenge and convey that idea more deeply into the subconscious mind.

A bit of science is also added throughout the book, intended to nourish that rational part of the brain that may be asking "how or why" this initiation can be so powerful. This information will include insights into psychology and neurology, and even touch upon powerful "occult elements" whose mysterious and mystical effects on reality are often difficult to fully explain in common language.

There is also a thread of hidden significance running throughout each challenge and throughout the initiation itself. You may find your-self suddenly becoming aware of the connections between certain ideas or even notice a new consciousness dawning within you—a mythic awareness and sublime understanding building with the momentum of each step of initiation.

At each gateway, or phase of development, there is a challenge that will include: an action to take, something new to consider, a decision to come to, or an affirmative statement to make regarding an impor-tant personal realization. Beneath each of these is something of deeper symbolic significance in the form of a mysterious riddle to be deci-phered by the subconscious mind as it engages in the ritual of mastering each challenge.

Think of the gates as portals of transformation. The ritual of going step-by-step through each gate and conquering each attending chal-lenge is also a process of gaining strength, as each challenge is an evolu-tionary exercise whose momentum builds throughout the initiation. At the successful completion of each of the nine challenges, a certain power will be gained. With time it will grow into a form of demon-strated mastery that we shall call Spiritual Kingship.

It's important to note that from the most ancient times initiation has been a process one undergoes in silence and secrecy. However, if you find it necessary to converse with someone you trust about your process, certain keywords have been added to provide some foundation to discuss what otherwise may be too difficult for the uninitiated to grasp.

On silence and secrecy, it's often the best policy to complete the initiation without drawing much notice from others or attempting to discuss it. Just like a butterfly in a cocoon or a fetus in utero, it's best to complete the process in a space separate from interference. Once completed, a person is free to discuss their experience with those who seem capable of understanding, but during the nine challenges, there is much to be gained from holding a perimeter of secrecy about what you are discovering about your Secret Self.

One of the great things about this self-initiation is that as a person undertakes its challenges, they are also learning its process, and that process has a way of continuing to work behind the scenes even when a person is not consciously thinking about it.

The process of this initiation is also circular, which means that it is ever-renewing. Completing the nine challenges brings one back to the beginning to repeat the process, but with the added perspective of previous experience, the person now enters again on a higher plane. At the same time, the strength and insight gained from earlier success make it possible to delve deeper into the heart of the matter, which yields even greater purity of realization and power of True Will.

Briefing

> "The Call" is the consummated love of a
> factual and poetical truth.

Within these pages the reader will be taking part in a ritual of the inner dimensions, seeking to decipher the riddle that lies at the heart of their very own being. During this symbolic quest, the Individual is challenged to overcome nine distinct tests, as they discover a path to their divine destiny via their True Will, and within its truth will find the basis for tapping into the profound, archetypal energies of Spiritual Kingship.

This book initiates its readers into the Self-unknown, inviting them to "read between the lines," and decipher their own Solar Myth. With self-made torch in hand, the Individual descends into an internal labyrinth to engage in a self-initiation modeled on secret, ancient rites.

"The Call" represents the resurrection and celebration of these timeless ancestral mysteries. Its song reawakens an eternal heritage inside the very DNA of the reader. It is the activation of these deeply unconscious, inherited instincts that will prompt the Individual to accept a series of mighty challenges and emerge from these ordeals triumphant.

The purpose of completing this circle of initiatory experience is for the Initiate to return changed, empowered, and with a clear understanding of both their own True Will and the cosmic nature of their evolving destiny. A vital part of this ritual process is what we shall call the "Centralization of the Psyche," which is a culmination of inner organization (or enlightenment) that develops as the reader learns to align themselves with the holistic intelligence of the Sun within. It's this epic, mountaintop attainment that opens the door of perspective to a previously hidden reality, where at last, the Individual may claim the scepter of their own "Divine Right."

The birth announced by "The Call" is equally the birth of a new Sun, and the birth of the Sovereign Individual whose Crown, Throne, and Kingdom are the first establishment of the Individual's True Will in the World.

This great rite, whose gathering momentum leads to the Crown of Individual Sovereignty, unabashedly sets the aim of its aspirations into the heart of a self-deifying solar mythology. In language both explicit and subtle, The Call's siren song illustrates the consummated love of a factual and poetic truth—the reality of Spiritual Kingship.

True Will, Divine Right & the Sovereign Individual

Sovereignty is understood as the full right and power to rule over oneself and one's conditions. To this end, it is technically defined as absolute, supreme, and unlimited power within one's realm. Thus, it follows that there is no power higher than the Individual who has attained the "Sovereign State."

The Sovereign Individual claims their divine right and becomes the source of their own spiritual law. There is no other earthly power higher than the Sovereign; there is no mortal who can issue commands to them. The Sovereign is hence the source of their own inner law. But what then is this Law? The answer: The Law of True Will, the legitimacy of the Individual's divine right.

True Will is the Sovereign's calling, it's the law that emerges from the heart. This law, True Will, which the Sovereign Individual serves, is also the purpose for which the Individual exists. In its purest sense, the True Will of the Individual is an echo of the True Will of the Universe. Its law is, for the individual who possesses it, the supreme and inevitable reason for their existence. This law also embodies the most absolute liberty as it represents freedom from the illusion of being something you're not. At the same time, this freedom bestows upon the Individual the ultimate authority over their own life.

Sovereignty is the foundation of a magical and spiritual life. Its Crown emerges from the still waters of meditation, a meditation that reveals the true constitution of the Individual and the essential divinity of their True Will. The Sovereign is anointed, it is the God of the innermost Self that grants autonomy. This Will-God is the ultimate spiritual authority in the Sovereign's life, no other can control them. If the Sovereign submits to the authority of another, they cease to be a Sovereign.

The Sovereign's existence has a divine purpose, and it is embodied in the calling of their True Will. The Sovereign commits to living their True Will, but nothing more. The Sovereign has a purpose, a higher calling, and to that purpose alone their powers as Sovereign are directed, and limited.

To be a Sovereign is to know one's True Will, and to know one's True Will is to have a purpose. This purpose is the source of the Sovereign's power. The Sovereign who possesses powers also possesses duties. They are the duties inherent in purpose, ultimately a duty to True Will. However, in the case of True Will, the duty is often in the form of a duty to one's liberty. The Sovereign must hold fast to that duty, in essence granting themselves the liberty to do their True Will, and nothing else.

The duty of the Individual is to live by the law of their own True Will. It is their communion with God, the Gods, the Universe, the Source, the Divine, the Self, Nature, etc. This True Will is deeply connected, one might even say it is identical to the Individual's "I AM."

It is because "IT IS," not because it ought to be, is supposed to be, should be, or would be more practical if it were otherwise. To this Sovereignty of True Will, the Individual must accept no interference, internal or external.

Moons orbit planets, as planets orbit the Sun. Likewise, a lesser Will is bound to get caught in the organizational gravity of a greater Will, becoming its orbiter. This is simply a feature of spiritual physics and its essential relationship to cosmic law.

It's the task of the Sovereign Individual to become the Sun of their own solar system. To do this, their consciousness must be able to maintain its freedom from external influences. They must not permit themselves to be pulled off course by the "will" or gravity of some other object. They must be able to proceed along their own course without wobbling. Once pulled off their path, they are no longer a Sovereign, just another fool aimlessly wandering in the World.

It's the person who loses contact with their True Will who's in danger of getting caught in the gravitational orbit of some other, more forceful presence. Whatever lacks its own gravitational center will naturally seek that stability outside itself, thus becoming an orbiter, and a follower of a gravitational law not its own. Without the stabilizing guidance of True Will, we are constantly in danger of being mastered by the strong will of another, of submitting to an external force whose center of gravity exceeds that of our own.

True Will is direct communion with the divine. The Sovereign's power comes from their adherence to True Will. The Sovereign cannot serve two wills at once. Sovereignty is indivisible; it cannot be divided into parts. Its nature is unity, and it is this sublime unity that its existence bestows upon the Sovereign.

Division within one's kingdom is a result of incongruence within one's being. The nature of the Crown is to be whole and undivided. The divided are easily conquered. The essence of the Will is its one-pointedness. Once it's divided it's no longer a will. To break a Will, divide it.

LAPIS EXILIS

Welcome to The Collegium

When a person enters upon this path of True Will and Sovereignty, they're now treading upon the same ground as many Great Individuals who have come before them. There is a Collegium of Immortals, an alumni of Kings in whose presence we walk. This path, the Tao of Kings, is of the most ancient origin. Its roots predate the pyramids. All of the lush foliage of civilization has been nourished by the primal roots of Sacred Kingship. When we enter the Collegium, we take up the torch of this most ancient of traditions.

Wisdom lives in the bright halls of the Kings. There the flame is kept alive; there the feast is taking place. Like Valhalla, the walls are made of spears and the roof of gilded shields. It is a place of conquest, of spirit, a place where the lives of mortal men are immortalized. It is this sacred fraternity whose initiation we seek in *The King's Curriculum*. This path, gilded in blood-spattered gold, is the path of the self-actualized man. In this place, one can hear both the hymns of divinity and the clashing of swords. It is here that the spirit who accepts the greatest challenge of life, the challenge of Spiritual Kingship, resides in eternal glory. The brave, the bold, the enduring, the conquering, the victorious—it is here that they sip from golden cups.

This is a path in which one must be initiated. It is a call that is within the blood. It is here, in the company of greatness, that we consider the purpose of our lives. How will we establish our own place amongst these God-Men? How will we go about living up to our full potential? To what great deeds will we strive, to live and die in pursuit of our own Immortality?

What is the "The Call?"

The Call is the siren song of Self. It is the voice of the Holy Father who is King reminding his Son, the would-be sovereign, of his divine right, his True Will. The Call gathers in the blood, an ancient strain of DNA brought to life. To those who have ears, let them hear. This voice is the creative will, it yearns to manifest. It manifests the Individual's subconscious will, which is a will-to-become, a secret message from the Individual's "I AM."

The Curriculum

Throughout ancient history, there were tutors to both heroes and Kings. The spiritual leaders of that time understood the importance of preserving the traditions and skills of a heroic nobility, and much time was dedicated to the instruction of rulership, its rituals and its curriculum. Among these teachers were Chiron, the mythological centaur who trained the hero Achilles, Aristotle who instructed Alexander the Great in both philosophy and art, and the magician priest of the Egyptian temples who counseled the Great Pharaoh Ramses in both the art of Sovereignty and the sacred ritual-transformation (like Alexander) of a Man into the spirit of the Sun-incarnate.

The Curriculum is twofold. On one hand, the Individual must attain the spiritual aptitude to claim their Sovereignty (Know Thyself) and exercise their Will so that they are living by the ethos of internal truth and righteousness. On the other hand, they must be "world-wise" to survive and thrive amongst those who may not look favorably upon a new King. Rather than expecting the World to applaud your ascension, you must instead prepare yourself to meet forces that will work against you, forces that will seek to perpetuate your servitude, constrict your Will and inhibit your expansion. The World is full of resistance. It is in the crucible of initiation that hidden weaknesses are exposed, and hidden strengths revealed. In this way, the ordeals of life help nature to separate the slag of slavish material from the forge of Kings.

To make one's way in this world it is essential to not only know where you are going but to also be able to get there, and that involves overcoming obstacles, outwitting opposition, and living up to the challenges required of a King. These skills involve the basics of what we shall call the Royal Arts, skills rarely developed amongst common men. It is to the task of resurrecting these skills that *The King's Curriculum* dedicates itself. With the migrations of humanity, the blood of this calling now circulates unconsciously in many individuals, the Collegium recognizes many new Kings may now spring from humble beginnings.

Blooming forth with new vigor, this path of initiation is now opened to a new generation of Spiritual Kings. It is beckoning those unique and timeless Individuals capable of hearing "The Call" to step forth from the common men and take their place amongst the Immortals. This lost art of Spiritual Kingship, this alchemy of human spirit that sustained mankind from its origins, is the heartbeat of The Collegium, a fraternity whose curriculum works to renew the world through the archetypal energy of the Sacred King.

The Initiation

To initiate is to begin. The Mission of this initiation into Spiritual Kingship is to realize your utmost potential and to serve it with everything you have. What stands between the Individual and this potential are the Nine Challenges. Like unfolding chapters in a book, each building upon the other, the Nine Challenges of initiation tell the story of the Individual becoming King. During this transformative journey, a person confronts some of the most basic challenges of human existence and meets them with the spirit of a conqueror. It is at each of these nine gateways that the Individual is strengthening their Will, mastering some skill, and moving forward to attain those priceless treasures of Sovereignty: namely, the Crown, the Throne, and the Kingdom.

The Threshold

There exists a mysterious, yet potent force within each Individual. A force of such power that for most of human history, the processes capable of revealing it have been fiercely guarded by those few who have known of its existence. Revered by a variety of names throughout history, its essence is essentially the same—through a ritualized initiation an Individual is able to tap into some force behind the veil of ordinary understanding, a force whose activation will reveal to them their True Will, a divine calling and path capable of leading their consciousness to the heights of being.

What is this enigmatic power called True Will, and how does a person manage to follow this sublime path when so many people struggle to even make it through their work-a-day lives?

This book outlines a process of self-initiation intended to assist a person in understanding and aligning with their True Will, a process that can lead them to transform their being into a reflection of their Truest Self. This Self-Initiating process will lead the Individual through nine challenges essential to the development of Self-Sovereignty and the attainment of True Will.

By following the path of initiation into a wholly internal landscape—a terrain whose contours are a reflection of their subconscious world—the Individual begins an epic journey that leads challenge by challenge into the heart of their own true spiritual constitution.

What this book can reveal to those with the courage to be honest with themselves and bold enough to affirm what they find, is no less than a knowledge of and communication with the Secret Self whose "Call" is the Individual's subconscious Will. Here they find a reality nourished by their own deepest and purest source of motivation and joy—the True Will.

Much like the alchemical processes of purifying lead into gold, this book outlines a method for discovering True Will as well as for readjusting one's initial self-discoveries so they may continue to evolve through inevitable life changes. This circular fluidity allows those capable of attaining inner alignment to also navigate their evolution through the culmination of different developmental phases, so they are able, time and time again, to initiate the beginning of new life chapters.

You are about to begin a powerful process, moving through successive cycles of initiating challenges. This process is designed to assist the Individual in bringing psychological wholeness into awareness. This is done with an interest in fulfilling what Jungian psychology calls "the requirements of Individuation." Everyone desires permission to be themselves. True Will is this siren song of Self, which the Sovereign Individual is called to answer. It is futile to resist destiny. What lies ahead is destined, though still unknown. The message of this book is a message of wholeness.

"In so far as every Individual has his own inborn
law of life, it is theoretically possible for every man
to follow this law before all others."

-Carl Jung

Full Disclosure

You are now approaching the threshold of transformation. Soon you will be presented with a choice, which you will either refuse or accept. The choice you make will depend on whether or not you hear "The Call."

If you do, you will step past an old boundary, accept a series of mighty challenges and finally prevail as a New Sun rising on the horizon, a Man transformed into a King incarnate. Passing through this threshold is like crossing the Rubicon…it is bold declaration of an intuited destiny.

The gates of this pylon lead into a vast internal labyrinth that lies within your own consciousness. This journey is a journey of becoming, a metamorphosis of a man into a King. What is the difference between these two creatures?

At present, a "man" (in the general sense) has become what Nietzsche called "the last man," a mere shell of the potential possible for himself. A "King," on the other hand, represents the heightened development of a Man into a creature capable of surpassing the limitations ordinarily attributed to the species.

A King is a Man who: is slave to none, who knows himself, is capable of free willed decision making, is willing to sacrifice that which he no longer needs for that which is now appropriate to his development; he is a man who can overcome obstacles, outwit opponents, survive amongst disorder, who establishes his own order, who is an authority unto himself, who is congruent in his actions, who is master of some craft or skill, who lives by the ethos of his True Will, who commands a grand vision, and who understands the immortality of his "I AM."

This Man to become King is one who hears "The Call" of initiation, who can already sense its necessity. This Man does not need to be convinced of these things, nor does he need to be converted to this path because he already recognizes its truth in his heart, already feels its potential in his blood, and already hears its "Call" as the voice of his own True Will heralding him home.

THE NINE NOBLE CHALLENGES, PORTALS OF TRANSFORMATION

1.) Beginnings and Endings

This represents a recognition of the eternal cycle of creation. Its image is both a gateway between two pylons and a snake with its tail in its mouth. At this early stage, the Initiate learns to part with things they have outgrown in order to liberate the energy necessary to bring to life what they now need.

2.) Quest for something New

This stage challenges the Initiate to behave in a way inconsistent with their habitual patterns, allowing them to activate the brain's frontal lobe and develop new neurological branches. This is necessary to the development of freewill decision making and is essential for out-maneuvering "the Phantom," a name given to the amalgamation of autonomous impulses, habits, and conditioning that conceal the Individual's True Nature and Will. The Phantom is a faceless silhouette, the image of this second challenge is a windswept desert, vast and wide.

3.) Know the Seed-of-ThySelf

The image of the Seed-of-Self is a golden seed inside of concentric spiral rings. These rings represent the layers of conditioning and societal modification that distort an Individual's conception of their True Self. The rough outer rind that encapsulates and protects this seed is the Individual's persona, a mask worn to deceive others and to guard this vulnerable seed against attack. However, as time passes this same mask can deceive its wearer, distorting their understanding of their True Nature and acting as a blind to one's own "True Self."

4.) Cultivate a Mythic Story

Most people are defined and confined by what we will call "an old-limiting story." It is a recitation of chronological events with a personal interpretation (often quite emotional) which concocts a meaning of those "facts" and consequently plays an enormous part in the construction of the Individual's Self-Concept. To break out of this constraint and into a new expansive horizon of Individual becoming, it is necessary to be able to take command of this creative process by becoming the author of one's own life, which means creating a personal myth unbound by the constraints of previous experience. The "New Constructive Myth," is an intentionally crafted, mythic story that represents a deeper, more significant, more resourceful truth that lies behind the old-limiting story. Its purpose is to define the universal theme for the Individual's life that reflects the self-chosen beliefs and values that are necessary to bring one's True Will to life. Its image is the sovereign flag of True Will that arises from the Seed-of-Self.

5.) Construct a Ritual of Inevitability

The purpose of the ritual of Inevitability is to cultivate the Seed-of-Self. Its image is a wheel whose axle is the hand that manifests the Individual's "I AM." The Ritual of Inevitability involves establishing a daily routine of developing resources and skills that will enable the Individual to master the challenges required by their values. To set this ritual in motion, the Individual must first identify their gift, making sure that their daily actions align with their professed intent. This phase represents an evolution of habit, committing to the development of one's gifts, generating momentum through the repetition of the particular daily habits and routines that will inevitably lead to the development of the Individual's True Will. This phase is about transforming thinking into being, designing one's day as a ritual in which the Individual's actions align with their primary intent.

6.) Climb your Primordial Mountain

The image associated with this phase is a primordial mountain whose highest peak wears a Crown. During this challenge, the Individual is learning to spiritualize their mission, honing down on the central objective of their existence and applying concentrated energy and focus to achieving its summit. This involves a process of internal organization which we will call "The Centralization of the Psyche." The mountain itself represents the unwavering strength that is born of this process. It represents the internal unity, the stability, and order that comes from connecting with the primordial foundations of Self. This challenge calls the Individual to extract the Gold-of-Self, which includes the Individual's True Nature, Mission, and Objective and embodies these in a mantra that both identifies and connects them with their Mythic Self and its driver: The True Will.

7.) Attain a Meta-Vision

The image for this phase is "The EYE" in a hovering triangle above a truncated pyramid. It represents the wholeness of the Individual's mission as a Grand Vision. To succeed in this challenge, the Individual begins the practice of mentally rising above a situation while keeping their Grand Vision in mind. This Higher (Disassociated) Vision allows for an expansive and far-reaching state of consciousness. This ability releases the Individual from those impediments born from a "ground-level perspective"; that point-of-view locked in perpetual blindness of circumstances and reactions. Attaining a Meta-Vision will grant the Individual the ability to rise above immediate events and "see the bigger picture," thus allowing them to foresee and strategize.

8.) Contact your Inner Initiator

The Inner Initiator represents the presence of the creative Self, a sort of transpersonal guidance or inner authority. The challenge in this phase is to connect with this experience of internal wisdom and to remain congruent with it. Attaining this "state" means the Individual is given the power to walk into the unknown with faith. Its related image is a hexagon and its primary quality is the manifestation of what psychologists call "synchronicity."

9.) Accepting the Unknown SELF

This last gate represents the Individual's completing of a level of purpose and the acceptance of the unfathomed possibility that still lies ahead. This phase calls for an all-encompassing openness to experience and the development of a personal sense of destiny, mystery, and mastery of transformation. It represents the ultimate reality revealed through the process of initiation: that life evolves through a series of stages, each one not quite what was expected, anticipated, or hoped for. This phase brings the Individual's awareness to reflect on a vital truth: that what they sought out to achieve or become was a process begun from a place of ignorance, from a lack of that particular experience. Now, having secured that experience, the Individual inevitably finds themselves "informed," and as such becomes aware of the flaws in their previous conception. This requires that they consider a reappraisal and modification of their original strategy and ultimate objective. In short, they have grown in wisdom, and this growth has revealed the misconceptions inherent in their previous undertakings. It is now necessary to release previous assumptions and move back into the dark folds of a new creation. In this way the circle completes itself. One finds themselves back at the beginning, the gates of initiation renewed, preparing to start a new journey. In this way, both life and initiation go on, and on, and on.

LAPIS EXILIS

INITIATION

CHAPTER ONE

Endings and Beginnings

"...we shall let the reader answer for himself: who is the happier man, he who has braved the storm of life and lived or he who has stayed securely on the shore and merely existed?"

-Hunter S. Thompson

Calling all brave men to the rigors of initiation:

The threshold of Initiation marks the boundary that affirms a cycle of change. It effectively marks the end and the beginning of a stage of development. Without the power of endings and beginnings things drag on past their time, their decay infecting the newness of the moments to come and stifling one's attempt to start afresh.

In the spiritual practice of ancient Egypt, there existed a God, Osiris, who embodied this force and this potential to start afresh by springing to life again and again from death and decay.

Initiation is a force of renewal. Without this force, life stagnates, yet when properly understood by the Initiate, this force possesses the power to transform life out of death and new beginnings from worn-out endings. To move from an ending to a new beginning requires a sacrifice of existing problems for new answers. Properly performed, initiation is an energetic upgrade, an evolution and renewal of life. It is the sprouting of a branch of fresh foliage from an ancient and established root.

The Art of Sacrifice Implies the Exchange of Something Lesser for Something Greater.

Initiation is approached through the gateway of the pylon. The pylon of Initiation is a gate with markers that represent a line of entry and departure. You went through this gate at birth, and you greet it again at death. It is both the entry into the tomb and the exit from the womb, simultaneously. The path that leads to it and through it is the path of life. This path is sometimes windy, often uphill, and quite mysterious in its paradoxical lessons. This path can feel both familiar and unknown, forgotten and remembered, personal and universal all at the same time.

Birth and death are both initiations; they are a time of separation and renewal.

The Womb Leads In and the Tomb Leads Out.

Initiation is a final break from the past, which means it's also the completion of a previous level of purpose and an affirmation of the unknown that lies ahead. To begin, the Initiate advances into the unknown, making a symbolic descent into their own mythological underworld. For many, this is a strange place inhabited by forces unknown and blocked by mysterious and unruled parts of self, as well as being the abode of humanity's collective fears. Here fierce threshold guardians make their threats, seeking to test the coherence of the Individual's will.

In ancient times, initiation was understood to be a heroic undertaking. Successfully passing through initiation meant that one had become a dragon-slayer, a hero in a world of living symbols. Metaphorically, this means seizing the treasure and rescuing the princess, but the ordeals of initiation itself are real. They involve a symbolic confrontation with death and an astute acceptance of endings and beginnings. This is the first demand of initiation, and one of the most important because its power is foundational.

Q: Why must the Initiate be willing to symbolically die? Why have so many of the ancient myths and mystery religions been built upon the idea of being slain?

A: Because for the Initiate to realize their utmost potential and serve it with everything they have, it's necessary to abandon the fear of loss so that they can focus all their energy on what they have set out to attain.

Once the Initiate understands the power of endings and beginnings, they have a greater ability to master change. For them, death becomes just a passage, they see it as an ending leading to a new beginning. For them, the fear of change disappears. Without this fear, they can embrace change, and even move boldly toward it. When confronted with change, the hero knows that the most effective response is to follow the wisdom of the heart.

Is it Not Better for Things to Die than for Them to Cease Being Born?

In this quest called life, we each advance toward that decisive moment when we will face death.

Initiation teaches us that the only death that can occur is a death of a part and not of the whole.

Those parts that *can* die are only the parts that have outlived their purpose, are outdated, and have become cumbersome. Their death means that the Initiate is free to revel in the renewed energy of a new life. With this perspective, they can come to understand the death of those decayed parts of self as a good thing. In this way, they are able to understand the process as a sort of alchemy of consciousness, whose momentum is carrying them forward in the direction of their highest visions. Like the alchemist, this Individual is involved in a life of transmutation, and from the dross of ordinary life is extracting the gold of SELF, which is the unique and original essence of each individual spirit.

In the beginning, the problem for most people will be internal resistance, and that resistance is identified as a sort of psychological inertia. It is this same unconscious gravity that pulls the Individual to the gates of Initiation, and for many, it's a point often preceded by a period of personal conflict.

Imagine this first gate of initiation, this pylon, like a line drawn in your mind. A line which you're now willing to move past. Symbolically stepping past the threshold means *the decision is made*. In doing so, the Individual affirms they are willing to sacrifice all that they know for all that they do not know. The process of initiation mirrors death and birth itself, and for the Individual, it is fundamentally a break with any belief in going backward.

This need for separation is the first challenge the would-be Sovereign faces. At first, they may feel a sense of loss, finality, and death; the same darkness before the dawn described in religious writings. And so, this willing ending becomes, in the moment after, the beginning of a new epoch of Self.

Some sense of personal conflict is required to spark the quest. Sometimes it's preceded by a rupture, like the tower card of the tarot deck, in which the structures one has built collapse. That's to say when the model of the world that an Individual constructed comes tumbling down.

Initiation is serious Juju; it sets hidden things in motion. It symbolizes both an acceptance of life's journey and a willingness to engage in its battle. Deciding to enter through this pylon is deciding to see its path through to the end. Like putting on gloves and stepping into a ring, initiation is an unspoken understanding of the nature of what one has decided to engage in. It acknowledges the possibility of a bloody battle ahead, as much as it acknowledges the glints of golden light streaming from that divinely coveted chalice that symbolizes victory. This victory represents the attainment which the Individual believes is their destiny. Ringing the bell of initiation is the sound of commitment, a penetrating sound that shatters all previous commitments to any but the Individual's own immortal destiny.

Initiation must be chosen of one's freewill. It's an act of liberty in which the Initiate is courting the SELF. Beginning this initiation is a single act, yet it is a process that unfolds again and again over a lifetime. It is a golden glittering door full of promise and adventure. It is the conquest of your liberty—the expression of which is manifest in acts of realizing your utmost potential, your mission of purpose, and serving it with everything you have.

The very first step on the path is a challenge, as well as an affirmation of future challenges. Taking this step means formulating a difficult symbolic procedure that has the power to communicate to your unconscious mind that you are ready. What dragon will you slay? What deed do you vow to accomplish? What looming obstacle will you overcome?

Whatever you choose, it must be within the limits of your potential, but just barely. The best challenges test one's heart and require a stretch of one's character, one's abilities, and one's conception of what is possible. It is in the overcoming and completion of this self-chosen challenge that the Individual affirms to their subconscious mind through their conscious actions that, "Yes, this is a willed act born of love."

What Now?

The past and future unite, one dies and the other is born. There is no turning back and yet you will return to this threshold of endings and beginnings again and again.

Life is full of duality. When the left hand and right hand are put together it is a gesture of prayer, when the ending and beginning are put together it is a gesture of initiation. The joining of these dual functions is the essence of life. Breathing in leads to breathing out, the process continues as long as life continues. The end of night is the beginning of day, as the end of the day is the beginning of night. This idea is important because it hints at a deeper reality—the end of some behavior, pattern, or viewpoint awakens its replacement. Understand this: there are no dead ends, only elongated circles completing themselves again and again.

Fear of change or even fear of death is based on a fear of endings, but the very idea of an actual ending is foreign to the understanding of the subconscious mind. When a person wishes to change something about themselves or take up a new path, they may tell themselves, "It's over, no more of that, it's finished. I'm not doing that anymore." But the unconscious mind cannot interpret the instructions at a deeper level because its understanding is based on the circular methods of nature.

A person who wants to stop smoking or lose weight struggles against the resistance of the unconscious mind that neither wants to quit nor to lose because that would mean being a quitter and a loser.

It's subtle, but it's the way the subconscious mind works.

Yet, to be effective at communicating with a deeper part of oneself it is necessary to close the loop and to effectively transfer the energy from an older function to the renewed life of a newer function. In this way death is becoming a new life and change is becoming transformation.

You might be wondering what this has to do with True Will, but to get to True Will it is essential to first prep the ground where you will be digging, and the first two challenges are just for that. The problem for most people is giving themselves a fresh start from which they can reevaluate themselves.

Initiation means entering into a new world, and that means leaving behind an old one. How do you motivate someone by saying, "Yes, now it's time to die," even if death is a required part of every process of becoming? The unconscious mind does not want to die, neither does the conscious mind unless it knows that a new life, a greater life, is right beyond the threshold.

At this point, it may already be evident how crucial this idea is to the process of transformation, how one must approach the crossroads of initiation time and time again. The end of childhood is the beginning of adolescence, which ends with the beginning of the teenage years, whose end follows with the beginning of adulthood, just as the end of today is the beginning of tomorrow.

It's so simple, yet when we struggle to evolve in necessary ways it's often because we fear the end of ideas, beliefs, and ways of living that no longer serve us. Much of what we cling to may even be working against our best interest, all because of a fear of change, all because of a misunderstanding of the circular nature of existence. Old endings lead to fresh new beginnings.

When a person learns to initiate new beginnings, they're learning to construct loops of renewal in their mind, enabling them to transform themselves, fearlessly recycling outgrown beliefs and behaviors. This circulating of energies is basic to the law of the conservation of energy, a law also reflected in consciousness.

Knowing this, a person who once subconsciously feared losing weight can reconstruct their internal model so they're saying to themselves, "The end of this excess body weight is the beginning of being fit." Rather than harboring fears of loss, the mind understands that it is an exchange of something unwanted for something desired.

This is a snapshot of initiation itself. One of the first skills developed during initiation is "The Sacrificial Upgrade." Its essence is learning the art of exchanging what's outmoded for what's presently appropriate to your needs.

Upgrading, in this way, is evolving. Evolution implies change, and every time an organism evolves it also loses something; a tail, claws, back hair, while it gains things such as upright mobility, opposable thumbs, or the ability to fashion durable clothing.

Considered in this way, initiation embodies an exchange, an upgrade. It becomes a means of personal evolution. This transformative process is designed to assist the conscious and unconscious parts of the mind to convert the energy liberated from the death of false wills, false paths, and un-resourceful beliefs for new uses.

To master endings and beginnings means we understand definitive boundaries. It gives us the ability to determine exactly where and when change is occurring. Rather than being the victims of arbitrary change, initiation teaches us to utilize it for our own ends, to further our Will. We become attuned to the precise point where one thing becomes another, and we attain the clarity to accurately estimate the value of that exchange. With this astute power of discrimination, the Initiate is better able to determine that fine line where one thing ends, and another begins. Metaphorically, this is our sword of critical reason.

Where does a thing stop being just a pleasurable habit and start being a dangerous addiction? When does dieting cease promoting well-being and start becoming an unhealthy obsession? When does memory stop being a just a sentimental fondness and start becoming an impediment to further development?

Initiation teaches us how to demarcate the line that defines one thing from another. It helps us to acknowledge the threshold that separates one phase of life, or project, from the next. In this way, we are able to disengage from past influences and identify with our new resolutions. This allows our mind to focus on things as they currently are.

With the mastery of this challenge, we learn to manufacture a feeling of "flow." We learn to unite all things into a seamless current of one becoming the other, changing and evolving eternally. This is one of the meanings of the ancient symbol of the ouroboros, a serpent with its tail in its mouth, the traditional symbol of initiation. It is a symbolic expression of the power inherent in the consciousness of the Initiate: the power to effectively distinguish change as it's occurring and effectively move with it, transforming as fluidly as water, adapting to life as it moves from season to season.

"...the snake that cannot shed its skin perishes..."

-Nietzsche, Dawn of Day

CHALLENGE:

Application for Self-Initiation

Endings and Beginnings

The basic concept: Initiation means to begin something. Every beginning is also an ending, and every ending is a new beginning. The first step is recognizing where the two meet and join together, uniting as one.

The Image: Ouroboros, the serpent with its tail in its mouth; a symbol of nature's infinite cycles of creation and destruction, life and death, and the eternal return. It is the magical symbol of the Initiate constantly recreating himself.

Action to take: The Sacrificial Upgrade, A sacred exchange. Examine yourself at this moment. What do you think or feel that you want right now? What you want will probably change, but for right now list five or so of your baseline desires, those things you wish to begin manifesting immediately. Once you've done that, consider what has gotten in the way of getting those things.

The Challenge: Often, a proper ending is the best way to instigate a new beginning. Relationships, habits, and styles need updating, and one of the best ways to do that is with "The Sacrificial Upgrade."

Bring new energy to life by sacrificing those things whose time has truly passed. At first, this process might stir feelings of loss and finality, but soon those feelings are replaced by the reawakening of energy and vitality that recycles the old and feeds the new. It is the consistent recycling of energies that allows a person to reach ever-higher levels of initiated consciousness.

If this seems difficult at first, just ask yourself (in as close to bare-naked truth as you can muster) what you truly need in your life right now. Then ask yourself what you're willing to trade, to make room for it. Consider the most appropriate sacrifice, one where you can clearly distinguish the lines of connection between the ending of the old thing and the new life of what you now need. What are the habits, thoughts, feelings, moods, perspectives, or even relationships whose sacrificial end will liberate the energy necessary to facilitate the life of this new becoming?

To bring a new life into being, an exchange of energy is necessary. This idea is at the root of commerce. We exchange our time and energy for money and then exchange our money for things we want and need. For ancient cultures, this represented an essential law of the Universe and was reflected in their spiritual practices. If they asked their gods for help, they might offer wine, blood, or some other valuable gift in exchange. Even today if a friend does us a favor, it is generally understood that the favor will one day be returned. Life is an exchange, and this is true at a deeper psychological level as well. If there is something you want, consider what you are willing to offer in exchange. If you want to bring an end to some habit, ask yourself what you will start doing to fill that void. If you want to start something new, what will you sacrifice to liberate the appropriate amount of time, money, energy to attain it?

In the practice of the Sacrificial Upgrade, a person is becoming familiar with this ancient and universal concept. Through statements that outline a willing exchange, a person consciously completes the loop of endings and beginnings in their mind.

By completing the statements below, you can experiment with the idea of trading in what you've outgrown for what you now need. Once you experience the power of the Sacrificial Upgrade, you'll be ready more than ever, to part with what you've truly outgrown as an exchange for what you currently need.

"Every act of creation is, first of all, an act of destruction."

-Pablo Picasso

The end of _____

is the beginning of_____.

I willfully bring an end to _____

as I willfully begin_____.

With the end of_____

the beginning of _____ now commences.

The time of _____ has ended;

the time of_____ has now begun.

Goodbye_____,

Hello_____.

Ritual to perform

Ding! Now you're ready to officially begin your initiation, with a ritual. Depending on how familiar you are with ritual psychology the details can be tailored to suit your needs. The more emphasis and energy consciously put into a ritual, the greater the subconscious ripple, and thus the more profound will be its effects.

Most rituals begin with a certain standard preparation. Bathing or showering beforehand is a typical preliminary step. You want to be clean to symbolize that everything extraneous to this one objective has been removed. It's also common to choose apparel that effectively matches the mood you wish to evoke and will help to suggest a separation from ordinary life to the subconscious mind. Also, choosing rhythmic and repetitive music with the power to stimulate and heighten your emotions can be used to your advantage. In some traditions, the Initiate will drink an intoxicant from a cup or chalice in a symbolic way.

For this ritual, the main items required are just a bell and two long tapered candles, one red and one blue, set enough distance apart for you to pass between them. The bell is to announce to your subconscious mind that this is a new chapter of life, a new aeon of consciousness. The tapered candles will mark the symbolic gateway of the pylon. The line between them symbolizes the threshold of initiation. The red and blue are complementary opposites, the primordial fire and ice as the engine of the cosmos—they represent the initiation of a path that unites all polarities: of endings and beginnings, death and rebirth, heat and cold, expansion and contraction, yin and yang, activity and contemplation, left and right, pain and pleasure, internal and external, truth and fantasy, masculine and feminine, the earthly and the divine. The line between them also symbolizes the point where the serpent's tail is in its mouth, the crossroads of all duality.

The royal road of initiation will wind back and forth between these two poles. Imagine these candles each as a pillar-shaped obelisk tapering to a point. The two giant pillars are set apart forming a pylon, or gate of initiation. The threshold between them is like a rift in reality, separating all distinct things from each other. Once a person crosses this threshold there is no turning back, they will be initiating a process that must, in time, complete itself. Before acting, think deeply about the meaning of taking that first step because once taken it will set in motion the momentum of a transformation that will take on a life of its own. Initiation is death and birth, both of which are irrevocable events.

If possible, set up a mirror so you can watch yourself as you take this symbolic step, initiating this ending and new beginning.

You may allow as much buildup to occur before taking the actual step as you like. The action is totally symbolic. No matter how insignificant it might seem to set up two candles and walk between them, the potential effect that such ritual proceedings can have on the subconscious mind is immense. Ritual is the language of the subconscious mind, and the subconscious mind has a very profound impact on the reality that we experience and the life that we manifest as Individuals.

Sometimes, at first, a ritual seems to generate little immediate outward change, or the change is noticed as just a subtle difference. At other times it establishes an alteration in both mind-state and life direction that becomes immediately apparent. Either way, when performed with the proper state of mind this symbolic act is capable of flipping a hidden switch within a person's subconscious, and the mysterious karma of True Will Initiation will have been activated.

A Bit of Science

The law of conservation of energy in physics states that energy cannot be created or destroyed; it can only be transformed from one form or state into another. Scientifically speaking, "the total energy of an isolated system in a given frame of reference remains constant."

More simply put, a person is a system unto himself or herself.

A person's beliefs, behaviors, self-concepts; essentially all the stuff that makes them into what they believe they are, can be transformed again and again through the evolutionary guidance of True Will, and yet, they will continue to preserve the energy inherent to their system, i.e. True Self.

In essence, the Initiate comes to realize that endings and beginnings are just phases of transformation. Knowing this, they learn to overcome the fear that so often causes people to hesitate and stumble during life's pivotal moments of change.

True Will initiation is the necessary reconfiguring of personal energies that bring us into greater alignment with our subconscious ideal.

Something Mystical

Have you ever heard of a mystical rebirth? Death/rebirth initiations have been fundamental to almost all religions and can be traced back to the Osirian myths of ancient Egypt. The essence of almost all faiths follows its general pattern. Someone: a god, an Initiate, or a prophet, willfully dies, goes into death and defeats death by realizing that life is eternal and then resurrects back to life, completing the loop of initiation and ascending to a higher level of consciousness while becoming a model for those yet to triumph over the fear of that experience.

For millennia this was a central initiatory practice in ancient Egyptian temples. Various methods were used, including psychoactive drugs, to facilitate states of mind in which the Initiate transcended the bounds of ordinary reality to experience simulated states of death and rebirth that were capable of leading the Initiate to a spiritual awakening.

Initiation has always included a death/rebirth theme, but one of its primary benefits is that the experience so often leads a person to reconsider fundamental beliefs, thus allowing them to more consciously formulate new ones. Death is symbolic of the ultimate change and the loss of this fear means a person also loses the fear of change in general.

Rather than losing their lives, the Initiates of these mysteries gained a unique and powerful understanding of life's eternally cyclical process, instigating a knowledge with far-reaching consequences, and effectively provoking a transformation of consciousness.

Instead of doing what most people do, that is, clinging to and identifying with outmoded and erroneous belief systems, the Initiate who grasps the eternal truth of endings and beginnings through their death/ rebirth experiences becomes capable of willfully recreating themselves to fit new conditions. This is often impossible for those who fail to appreciate change because they still fear it as a form of death.

My Experience

At the start of my initiation, I spent most of my time looking backward, trying to overcome the past. I was habitually looking for redemption, retribution, and revenge. I reread the books I loved again and again until I knew them by heart. I anchored myself in history. When the time came to move on, I looked back at the glory (often imagined) of a world that had been, and I felt a longing for its return. The memory of past defeats and failures made me miserable.

Overcoming the past has represented one of my primary challenges. I've had a very difficult time making a break from it. Old loves, hates, memories and wounds would beg me not to let them go, so I held on to them, even the very painful ones as if they were sentimental knickknacks.

To cope I developed a host of self-destructive behaviors cloaked as self-soothing habits. Many of my thoughts throughout the day would take the same circular routes as the days and weeks before, and when I looked back at journal entries from ten years earlier, I found the same troublesome emotions still plaguing my pen. The ruts were obvious; I had worn trenches into my mind. In the earliest phases, escape seemed impossible.

When I first began to contemplate this idea of endings and beginnings, I made a list of several big-ticket items I was willing to trade for some new mind-states and wrote them down in what I called my Sacrificial Upgrade. When I look back at that list today, I can appreciate how challenging the task of separating from the past has been. Even after I officially decided to let things go, circumstances would seemingly contrive to make the separation almost impossible.

With some things, I felt I just couldn't let go. There was a sense of an empty hole whenever I got close to freeing myself. With some things, I struggled and felt like a failure. I wondered, "Can I forget this, can I let this go?" But with other things, merely writing them into my Sacrificial Upgrade had an almost magical effect. Whenever they came up, I put them down. Whenever my mind would wander to them, I would cut them off. Even when it hurt to let them go, I felt a masochistic joy in their banishment. With some things, I was ready to begin anew.

I dealt with this problem for some time. Even when I felt ready to go on to the next stages of initiation, I knew I had not yet mastered beginnings and endings. After a while, I put out of my mind any conflict about letting certain things go, and just continued with the initiation, albeit with a sense of lingering frustration. Some of these frustrations continued for a while, but whereas before I had been digging a deeper trench everyday with circular thinking and habitual behaviors, I now had developed the new habit of looking for ways to escape from my old ones. Whenever I failed to rid myself of something

I no longer wanted, there would be a little pain from failing, but also a renewed desire to escape the pattern. Eventually, I found that I could break free, although temporarily. More and more I started to associate freedom from those habits as instrumental to sovereignty. In time, I began to sense that the power was mine to decide what new routes to take. Then quite unexpectedly, I began to feel free.

Architects of True Will

During this initiation, you will be digging deep into your foundations, and the danger inherent in this is the danger of "arbitrary change." The change that initiation brings about is not just for the sake of change. It is not a rebellious reaction against the World, nor is it about reinventing oneself to fit current standards of social acceptability. It's much more than that. It's about re-aligning yourself with the fundamental nature of your True Self.

This means that the change is not just an updated reflection of a newborn fad or a whim of fancy. We are not trying to "reinvent ourselves" for the fun of it, as popular culture encourages. Instead, it's about seeking a conscious alignment with the deep-seated inner drive organically embedded in your subconscious mind and existing within your DNA.

True Will represents a deeply instinctive drive unmodified by society. Its essence is authentic, the experience of a sort of "higher calling." To discover it, we must be clear in our motives, and diligent in our appraisals so that we can attune to the true voice of our original selves.

To accomplish this, it's necessary to wield the sword of critical examination, and ask, "What higher cause do we serve? How does attacking a problem, in ourselves or the world, apply to the necessity of my life's calling?"

In the past century, values that have existed for millennia have been ripped to the ground, and yet the ideas that have sought to replace them rarely endure for more than a decade, a few at most, before crumbling. Have past revolutions failed because of shoddy workmanship, or just poor planning? In time, anti-establishment must give way to re-establishment.

It is no longer enough to just call for social reformation and to be a mouthpiece for the injustices of the past. Today there are more than enough angry mobs hell-bent on revenge and revolution. What humanity needs now is an abundance of practical dreamers capable of drawing up blueprints for a new future. The time of self-righteous revolutionaries is drawing to a close. Now is the time for the architects of True Will visions to dawn.

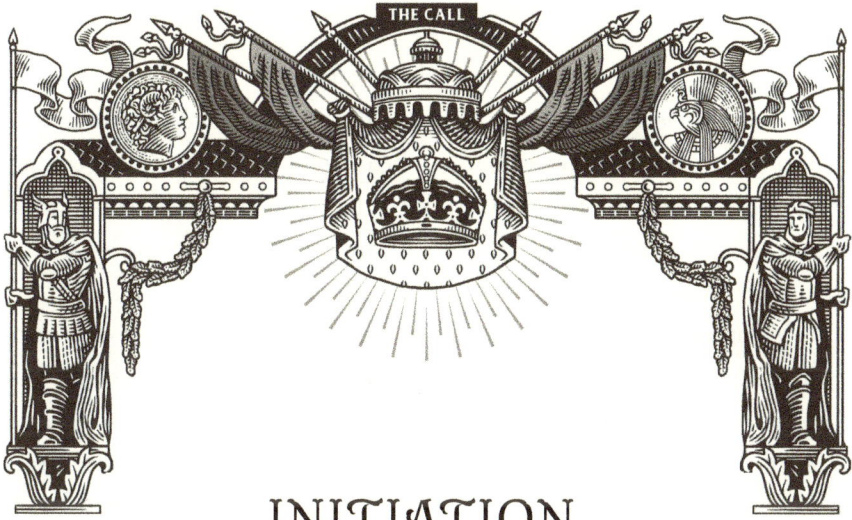

INITIATION

CHAPTER TWO

The Quest for Something New

"Imitation is suicide."

-Ralph Waldo Emerson

Passing through the pylon of initiation is like passing from one world to another, from one aeon to another, from B.C. to A.D. and beyond.

Having moved through the gate, you now notice yourself entering into a strange new land. This new territory is an emerging desert landscape where familiar landmarks become obscured, and wispy winds of change continuously erase one's previous footsteps. It appears, at first glance, that the god of this world is one of chaos.

In this desert, it's possible to discern small outcroppings of rocks that once towered as mountains. Now worn and weathered they're being reduced to sand, eventually to be claimed by the constant change and endless shifts of a remorseless desert spirit. It's here that mankind has come, again and again, in preparation to discover the hidden power of the self-unknown.

In the vastness of this desert all "shoulds" and "oughts" are engulfed. The emptiness of this desert shatters the coherent reasons of mind, it mocks at the so-called achievements of mankind. In its endless change, it retains its purity. Nothing can be written in the sand, all footprints are engulfed in its ceaseless movement, all direction is confused by its shifting dunes, all paths are consumed by its relentless renewal. In this place old habits, routines and patterns cannot exist.

All is consumed in constant newness; all evidence of old stories will perish by nightfall. In turn, the memory of last night's dream is banished by the first fierce rays of the morning light. This image, of a desert vast and wide, is a symbol. It's in the lessons of this symbol that we seek the power of new neurology.

Here the Challenge and Power are One and the Same: to be Able to do Something New.

When wandering through this unfamiliar environment the Individual is scrambling their physiological, mental, and emotional response patterns. During this phase, the Initiate is learning to behave in a way inconsistent with their previous patterns. In doing so, they are restructuring their neurological model of the world, a model that exists in the habituated patterns and pathways of their mind. It's in overcoming an unresourceful habit that the Initiate learns to enrich their internal model of the World. In this period of psychological renewal, a person learns to make choices based on present conditions rather than acting from the habit of automation. No longer are they blindly repeating tired formulas of thought and outdated strategies that stopped evolving long ago.

When we feel stuck in life, when the opportunities of the world seem dead, when all that's good has seemed to pass, it's because we are recognizing the death of "previous conditions." It's upon this recognition that the powerful habit of making new choices becomes our true ally. To activate this power, it's necessary to strike out in a novel direction and actively pursue something new. For the Initiate, this means discarding collections of experience that have been inhibiting the Will and its noble growth.

The problem with habituated actions is that they put an important part of the mind to sleep, the part of the mind responsible for freewill. Neurologists have discovered that novel actions, which form the basis of free willed decision making, activate the frontal lobes, which are the parts of the brain responsible for acts of creativity.

Changes in one's environment and habit effect an alteration in one's thought processes, and also the emotional reactions that result from those thoughts. The Individual who has enveloped himself in New Neurology can profoundly modify their world at a neurological level. As a consequence, their mind becomes capable of generating new types and degrees of thought, which means they begin experiencing new types and degrees of correlating emotions.

Q: How do we overcome the rutted conditions of habit and activate the sublime power of True Will?

A: By invoking New Neurology, by experiencing that which had previously lain outside our experience, by expanding our internal model of the world.

When an Individual performs actions that are neurologically new to them, they are activating, stimulating, and developing parts of the brain (the frontal lobe) from which arguably mankind's greatest gifts and creations have emerged. Consider this experiment in New Neurology as the stretch and warm-up before the exercise of True Will.

Once electrified by the novel stimulus, the brain's frontal lobe is awakened to life. As this happens the Individual gains clarity and sheds the distorted outer layers that have been clouding the awareness of their True Will up until now.

These layers are the accumulated debris of habituated patterns. Many of these patterns find their origin in unconscious childhood programming, memories of past events, traumas and emotional obsessions. These outer layers can also be associated with layers of what is sometimes called karma. The Individual, when developing the habit of New Neurology, discovers an effective way to work through this karma *in bulk*.

Often this process of clearing away past programming will arouse rebel thoughts and their accompanying emotions to threaten the Initiate's inner peace with their constant intrusion. It's from the inner turbulence created by such thoughts that the mind becomes exhausted. Many people suffer mental and emotional assault from their thinking processes or from externally embedded, viral thoughts with which they have become infected.

It's these compulsive thoughts that will seek to fascinate, allure, or distract the mind of the Individual so as to prevent it from claiming the godlike power of free willed decision making. Thus, binding it to "the Phantom."

But, when an individual becomes capable of claiming this power of free willed decision making, those slavish fetters are broken and the malignant forces of automation, viral programming and social convention become inert. Most well-mannered people would never suspect that it's their own "agreeability" that binds them to false purposes, that it's the desire for consensus that contaminates their True Will.

With the invention of new options, we need not labor toward dead ends. With the power of New Neurology, the Individual learns to use what's useful, discard what isn't, and make every moment their own by becoming awake to their true intention, and by being free willed in their actions.

"...creating, actualizing one's possibilities, always involves destructive as well as constructive aspects. It always involves destroying the status quo, destroying old patterns within oneself, progressively destroying what one has clung to from childhood on, and creating new and original forms and ways of living..."

-Rollo May, The meaning of Anxiety

The Phantom

The whole time the Individual is seeking this power of New Neurology they are being chased by the "Phantom" of their past neurological preferences. The old habits cry out, "Wait, love me again!"

But the Individual who turns back to love the Phantom turns their face toward death, who is yesterday and yesterday's patterns, who is a conglomeration of things learned, of things repeated, and of things of which one has become convinced. This Phantom is the force that tries to claim possession of the face in the mirror by stamping it with a particular story, and in this clever way manages also to stamp its effects upon the forming future.

This demonic possession of automation and habit is the Phantom Self—the enemy of sovereignty, the stealer of crowns, the usurper of thrones. The Phantom Self is the devil tempting forgetfulness of True Self, and its unconscious aim is the abdication of the Individual's freewill.

Courting this false self is an invitation to servitude, a chain around the neck called the slavery of habit. The Individual who wears it unconsciously expresses an inability to make free willed decisions, which is an inability to truly think for themselves. Thus, they are incapable of claiming their divine right, or possessing the power of authority over themselves and their own life.

The Phantom is a psychological stalker. Like a friend turned enemy, it knows the Individual's old habits, the routes they habitually take to work, and the spaces and places their body and mind habitually occupy. In these known locations the Phantom lurks. In known thoughts the Phantom lies quietly, preparing for an unconscious ambush.

"...divest the self of the false wrappings of the persona..."

-Carl Jung, The Relations Between the Ego and the Unconscious

---

THINGS TO CONSIDER:

We are born pure. Then we are socialized. Little by little we develop a personality, little by little the True Self learns to wear its mask.

It's from the Greeks that the word persona comes to us, a word meaning mask. This mask, or persona, is essential to the adaptation process that each person goes through in becoming an adult. The real problem is not that we learn to adapt our behaviors to match the appropriate social situation, the problem is that often by the time we are grown that "self" being portrayed by the mask becomes habitual, and what lies underneath has become a stranger. This feeling of becoming "a stranger to oneself" is what many of us resign to the process of growing up. But where does the True Self go?

Although always present, the True Self and its Will can become clouded by layers of conditioning that slowly insulate a person from their natural responses. Slowly the messages from within are muddled by intervening thought processes. Their censorship causes hesitation where once there was a pure expression and an innate intuition. What once roamed free as a child slowly becomes socially restrained.

We are trained to be considerate of other people, to moderate self-expression that may challenge others, may make them feel uneasy, give them a reason to feel offended, or feel insecure. Instead of just being true to one's Self, socialization modifies a person's natural energies so that free expression hesitates or even becomes neutered. In these cases, one's instinctual flow becomes restricted while it considers the possible social consequences of its natural impulses. Slowly the socialized Individual creates an internal customs agent to secure the border between their inner impulses and their outer expressions.

Despite the heavy cost this type of self-censorship imposes on the development of personal genius and true will, there exists an almost unanimous agreement that being nice and developing an agreeable and socially acceptable persona is essential to civilized life. Uncensored Individuals are seen as dangerous, yet censorship robs the Individual of their very individuality.

So how does a person who wishes to be true to themselves live in a society composed of many different types of people who might feel threatened by an uncensored True Will?

There is no easy answer, this one issue has driven many prophets into a desert wilderness, but for this initiation, the first step is for the Initiate to make a conscious break between their True Self and the mask they wear. What other people know of your True Self is of little consequence. It's only important that you know the difference between the mask of persona and the spirit that lives beyond it.

The first step of initiation was about endings and beginnings. The second is about peering behind the habits and patterns that make up the social mask for an unfiltered, first glimpse of True Will.

The Subconscious Mind

In this process of coming to understand oneself more deeply, one of the first enigmas encountered is that of the relationship between one's conscious and subconscious mind. We all know what the conscious mind is because it's everything that we know and are aware of. That leaves the subconscious or unconscious mind to rule over what we do not know that we know. A mystery indeed!

Q: How does a person regulate their blood pressure, grow hair, digest food, synthesize bones and regenerate cells?

A: Unconsciously.

A person is more unconscious than they can ever be aware of. Conscious awareness is just the tip of the iceberg, and yet the conscious mind is given the supreme task of directing the powerful unconscious forces that move below the water level of consciousness. So, what does that mean?

It means you have an unconscious mind and a conscious mind and it's very important that they work together. A person is wasting their energy if these two minds are incongruent. If a person's conscious Will opposes their subconscious Will they can never be effective, their energy is divided against itself. A person who suffers from an incongruence between the Will of their conscious and unconscious mind is suffering a metaphoric Civil War raging within their being.

True Will / False Will / Dead Will

As we talked about before, initiating True Will involves death and birth simultaneously. It's the death of the false will, and the birth of the True Will. The two cannot exist together. To signify our conscious intent to assume a new path, we prepare a special ritual to signify the exchange. Although this stage of initiation is just a moment in time, its effects ripple outward for all of eternity. It's something to consider because the act of initiating True Will is irrevocable.

Once the process begins, its natural momentum will want to carry on until completion. Any attempt to turn back after that means a person would be consciously attempting to stifle their own True Will. Many people have been trained to impede their natural development. Not only do they expend enormous amounts of their energy in resisting what is natural to them, but many are also convinced that sabotaging their True Will is the mark of a socially conscious person.

Many have been trained to subvert their inherent natures and instinctual impulses. They've been taught to believe that what comes naturally to them is unacceptable. Yet, a person who neuters their instincts or subconscious Will for a persona that fits current concepts of social acceptability puts himself at odds with his True Self.

As a result of these social modifications, True Will is forced to mask itself. Instead of experiencing the natural freedom of innate expression, we find ourselves contending with self-censorship and the deeper psychological ramifications and subconscious distress that have come to characterize post-modern society.

The more conscious a person is, the more responsible they are for what they do. If a person were to unwittingly hit a stray cat with their car it would be considered an unfortunate and regrettable accident, but if done consciously, it would take on a different meaning. Similarly, the thought of a person going through life only dimly aware they're on a false path is dreadful; but for a person who has awakened their True

Will to consciously decide to work against it means also committing an offense against the divine. With knowledge comes power, with power comes responsibility, and this very much holds to True Will.

This is another basic precaution with initiation to be considered because becoming conscious of True Will holds the same responsibility as the birth of a child. It is possible to take precautions against the conception of a child. There are ways to prevent it. But once a child is born, its life has a natural right to be and to develop, unto its completion. The same holds for initiating True Will. With much effort, a person can try to avoid it altogether, and many do just this. But once the process commences, a person's True Will takes on a life of its own. To oppose it or to try to terminate it once it's been born into consciousness and named is a dubious affair. To work against one's True Will is a type of evil.

On the other hand, the false will(s) must be rooted out and exterminated without mercy. However, this may not be easy. Even false wills have lives of their own and in most cases will not just lie down and die. They may even haunt the Initiate for a time in the form of "the Phantom." As previously mentioned, the Phantom is a name given to the amalgamation of complexes, habits, tendencies, fantasies, and automated behaviors that seek to reaffirm their control over a person's free-will decision-making process.

For example, a person who has recently made the conscious choice to quit smoking may find themselves unconsciously putting a cigarette in their mouth and lighting it.

A person new on the path of Initiation must outwit this phantom in the first stages by starving it of its habits.

CHALLENGE:

Application for Self-Initiation

The Quest for Something New

Basic concept: True Will is a living energy, based on no preconceived notions. It's beyond acquired conditioning, education or training. It lies beneath all of these, at the root of a person's being. To discover the living pulse of True Will it's necessary to clear away the accumulated clutter that's been obscuring the messages coming from deep within. To free oneself for this task, it's necessary to activate the brain's frontal lobes and liberate the freewill decision-making process from the "hindbrain's" automated response patterns.

The image: A desert landscape, shifting dunes remorselessly covering the tracks of every previously trodden path, a terrain without any known landmark. The Horns of Ammon.

The Challenge: Begin activating your brain's Frontal Lobe by subtly altering everything you do. Walk into the fresh landscape of New Neurology by taking actions you've never taken before. Develop the habit of doing something new.

Action to take: Behave in a way inconsistent with your patterns by cultivating novel choices that activate your brain's Frontal Lobe. Drive different routes, eat unfamiliar foods, use your non-dominant hand, meet different people, go to strange places, and wake up at odd hours as you indulge in a forty-day quest for a new experience.

Seek out "first times" as you begin pioneering new neurological experience. You are going where your Mind and experience have not gone before. The more you branch out into the unfamiliar, the greater "net" your Mind casts when it conjures insights and inspirations.

This challenge is about interrupting long-running habituated patterns and cultivating new choices as you explore ways to subtly alter how you do things. Exposing your mind to a novel stimulus can bring immediate rewards, including an awakening of your creativity and a rebirth of your lust for life.

During the forty-days of de-habituating yourself, a person is removing the outer layers of automation that are masking their True Will. Once completed, you are now primed to delve into your Core and discover the power of your authentic nature. Breaking the trance of automated behaviors allows you to awaken your brain's Frontal Lobe so that you are entering a creative state ideal for the next challenge.

Remember, before you begin penetrating the core of your Secret Self, you must first peel back the accumulated layers of conditioning that have surrounded that core and have been muddling and masking your True Will. Begin subtly altering everything you do as you practice gradually interrupting your long-running patterns. Keep an "expansion list" of the new experiences you are having, and any "first times" that occur during the next forty days. Keeping a journal is a great way to record the cause and effect relationship these novel experiences have within your consciousness.

A Bit of Science

Doing something new has some interesting connections with Neurology. In the past few decades, researchers have discovered how different areas of the brain perform different functions and respond differently to various stimuli.

For example, neuroscientists have noticed that very different parts of the brain are activated depending on whether or not a particular action has been routinely performed. When it comes to routine actions, something that a person does daily like brushing their teeth, the hindbrain takes over and allows the task to happen in a rather automated fashion.

Much of what we do, we have done before. In this way habits form, patterns of behavior take root, and automation sets in. When this happens, the hindbrain helps us disengage from the decision-making process and allows the learned behavior to run as a sort of program. In this way, we drive our usual route home without having to think much about it.

This tendency is useful to a degree and can serve an important function when we want to master some skills. Once we've done something enough times, we don't have to think about it anymore, and our mind is free to focus on something else entirely or even to just daydream. In this way, we strengthen the neural pathways that perform that action. As these pathways strengthen, the action becomes easier and easier until it becomes automatic.

However, if you want to connect with something as authentic as your True Will, then a life composed of automated response patterns just isn't going to cut it. The more routine a person's life becomes, the more the hindbrain will take over. Without the intervention of new neurology in the form of new stimuli, the hindbrain will tend to take a greater command over a person's neurological activity. Eventually, they find themselves rutted by repetitive, predictable neurological patterns. In a sense, when the free willed aspect of a person has been put to sleep, they've been effectively zombified. That's the influence of the Phantom Self.

To outwit the Phantom's influence, a person must train themselves to behave in a way inconsistent with their preexisting model long enough to develop the new habit. This conscious break with old neurological patterns reawakens the mind by forming new neural connections. In short, the best way to overcome the sleepy mood of the phantom is by doing something new.

Something Mystical

Why a 40-day challenge? Well, because the number 40 has historically held certain powerful, symbolic significance, especially in spiritual
matters. Scriptures talk of a Christ-figure who fasted for forty days in the
desert. The story of Moses leading the Hebrews is a story of wandering
for forty years through the desert. Muhammad was forty years old when
he first received his vision from the archangel Gabriel. The flood in
Genesis lasted for forty days and forty nights. Symbolically the number
forty represents the separation of two distinct epochs, and so we use it
here to separate ourselves from the past for the purposes of renewal.

Even the idea of "New Neurology" has links with spiritual tradition.
When a new monk joins a monastery, he will often shave his head, shed
his old clothes and say goodbye to his family before giving himself over
to prayer, ritual, and meditation. Why? To gain freedom, for a time,
from what is "usual" so that he can awaken specific parts of the brain
responsible for activating New Neurology. In this new state, his mind
is better prepared to receive the mystical revelations that are to come.

Neurologically, this is also a reference to what is known as the
Horns of Ammon, two elongated eminences on the floor of each lateral
ventricle of the human brain that simulate a horn shape, and which
regulate long and short-term memory and spatial navigation.

Mythologically, Ammon is the ram-headed king of the gods, the
hidden creator, the mysterious soul of the universe. When Alexander
crossed the desert on his way to the oasis of Siwa he was headed to the
temple of Ammon. There he was acknowledged by the Egyptian priest
as the son of Ammon, making Alexander the son of a God.

Later, Alexander was depicted on a coin with a ram's horns growing
from his head, a powerful symbol of divine rulership, a visual affirmation of his godlike power to break out of old patterns and defy expec-
tations. Thus, Alexander did what so often feels impossible to us: he
conquered stagnant conditions and established a new self-created order.

My Experience

When I first set my intention to complete the forty-day New Neurology Challenge I was pretty excited by the thought of all the novel experiences that lay ahead. What I quickly discovered, however, was that even when I set out to do new things, I found myself slipping unconsciously back into old habits. I would tell myself, "I'm taking a new route home today," and then a distracting thought would come to mind and the next thing I knew I had taken the same old route. Over and over I did this. Doing something new turned out to be more difficult than I thought. Not because I didn't want to do things in a new way, but because I had unconsciously programmed myself with certain patterns of automated behavior that set in as soon as my attention became distracted. Without constant vigilance, my default programs would take over and I would find myself acting like a robot.

During the first week, pulling myself away from the same old patterns was like trying to pull two magnets apart. It felt as if there was some invisible force that kept bringing me back to what I had sought to flee. During the second week, I managed to successfully divert myself into new routes, but when it came to new foods, I found myself rather reluctantly swallowing exotic spices.

By the third week, I was getting the hang of it, but the more I attempted to do something new, the more I became aware of how automated behavior dominated my life. I had never thought about it before, but almost everything I did was rooted in unconscious behavior patterns: the way I brushed my teeth, the way I greeted my children in the morning, the way I walked, talked, laughed, chewed, slept, it was all routine. Even my moods were predictable.

It wasn't until the last three days of the forty-day New Neurology challenge that I felt I had awakened into a new state of mind. It took that long to be able to see all the ways I was not truly living, not truly conscious, but just going through the motions of a pre-programmed state of being. Finally, on the last day, I realized that I had come a long way in identifying and overcoming that habituated "Phantom Self," and in doing so developed what was truly the best habit of all—the habit of doing something new.

INITIATION

CHAPTER THREE

Know the Seed -of- Thyself

"It is a seed that carries a fruit of its species within it."

-R.A. Schwaller de Lubicz, The Temple of Man

As you finish the forty-day crossing of that desert of change, you may notice a sense of "familiar emptiness." Your mind, now alive with new awareness, may proceed to stalk your inner truth like a hungered hunter whose nourishment comes from a single source. The purpose of those forty days was to shed the last "outer purposes" of life before the pylon. Now cleansed, there is but one current objective, to discover the Seed-of-Self.

For the last time, the Individual might cast a glance back across the expanse of that seemingly endless desert and reminisce upon what they've left behind. They might look back and wonder where "certainty" went. In this new land, everything seems different.

For the last time, they might momentarily consider running back to a memory. They might even consider giving up, until they realize, *there's nothing to go back to*. In truth, they would not have even begun this journey in the first place had there really been any more life back there in that old stagnation. For a moment, the Initiate might feel a sense of despair, a completely natural feeling in the face of the unknown.

Now standing here, far away from home, it may seem natural to wonder why we've abandoned ourselves to what *could be* just a foolish attempt? The Initiate may battle now with feelings of remorse, maybe even cry out in repentance, "Why was it not good enough? Why could I not just make myself happy under those old conditions?"

Possibly a fearful thought may briefly flash—"There *is nothing else* beyond this desert!"

Desperately their eyes may search for familiarity. Tears threaten. Weakness threatens. Panic threatens. The past is truly gone. The feeling is gripping, as if in one's mind an ocean liner is disappearing into a cold-black abyss from which nothing ever returns, loaded down with the cargo of all one is and all that one has loved.

Quelling this feeling can be quite difficult, but it's necessary, because it naturally prompts a person to embrace a decisive moment, in which they instinctively turn away from the path of the past, and away from a hope that is anything but ahead.

Stumbling out of this desert the Initiate may be feeling exposed, and raw, like an animal.

Here they discover the mask of persona is of no help. The self-assured promises of one's assumptions have now come into question. The persona and its restrictive limits, its ultimate utility, are clearly inadequate for what the Initiate is currently facing. Recent changes in scenery have revealed the persona to be nothing more than a fashionable illusion—like wearing dress shoes out into the rough wilderness. In this new terrain, the mind is quickly forced to distinguish between what is truly useful, durable, and functional in the world, and what is just a shiny loafer made for standing around and putting on a show.

Here the mind awakens to a challenging fact. There is no longer any realistic option of turning back on new discoveries. As the Individual looks forward, toward the road that lies ahead, they see it's long and that it ascends ever more steeply upward. Squinting in the emerging sunlight, the initiate begins to make out what looks to be green sprigs from the tops of trees, still quite a way off in the distance, somewhere on the new horizon. To get there, it's necessary to climb higher upward. As the Initiate approaches, they now see that this green patch of life sits far up on the sunny side of a large hill extending in front of the shadowy summit of an even larger mountain.

It's here and now that the Individual realizes they have some things to reconsider.

What's in Your Bag?

The story of the Tarot is the story of the journey of the Fool.

In the beginning, the Fool sets out on his journey of self-realization, with no idea where the journey shall lead, merely beginning with optimism, a loyal dog, and a small bag tied to a stick slung over his shoulder.

This is the depiction on the Fool card itself and it shows the naive face we all wear when we've yet to meet the World in its completion. In a classic version of the card, The Fool is shown at the beginning of his epic journey almost immediately stepping off the ledge of a cliff, his inattentive gaze cast up to the sky, most likely lost in the fantastic creations of his own ungrounded imagination. The Fool sees not the World, but the Fool's own foolish imaginings *about* the World.

It would be the early end of this Fool except for the fact that his loyal dog notices the cliff and warns the Fool in his doggish way, proving that the dog truly is man's best friend. This lovable beast represents the first stirrings of the "Inner Initiator's" mysterious, synchronistic guidance.

Saved from this near fall, the first stirrings of awakening begin in the Fool. It's here, too far beyond the past, and not nearly close enough to the future that the Initiate might find themselves sharing sentiments with The Fool. Like the meager contents of the hobo bag slung over the shoulder of the Fool, the quest now demands the Individual look at what they have *in their bag*. That is to say, what resources, skills, knowledge, abilities, and beliefs do they carry?

Alone and far from home, both the fool and the Initiate must face a sobering fact: in this position, what's required must either be created from, or mined out of, their very own being. In other words, with the past now gone, what shall the future be built of? What is available to begin the construction of this next phase?

In those first moments, both the Fool and the Initiate upon this path might find themselves naturally feeling some despair. They have arguably been stripped of all but their actual being, and with empty hands, they might find themselves feeling that perhaps they have nothing at all. But in truth, the things sacrificed at the start of the journey were merely those things that had outlived their purpose.

Equally, the Individual, having arrived in this strange land with nothing, must console themselves with the understanding that the rules that apply in this land did not apply in the desert. What's now required is not something they no longer have because they had to give up, but instead, it is something they require because *they've yet to achieve it*.

What this means is that movement can only be forward. The stage is set. It's time to begin: to discover, to claim, and to conquer this next phase of becoming. What the Initiate knew, or maybe even just thought they knew (before the journey began) does not even apply to these new conditions.

You Got What You Have, You Have What You Are, Now What Are You Going To Do With It?

This seems to be both the realization and the question at hand, except for the fact that the essential variables are still missing.

Does the Individual know what they really have?
Does the Individual know who they really are?

Without this knowledge, can the Individual really know what they are capable of, or what they're going to do with it? At this point, we might find ourselves looking into the mirror and be truly perplexed, thinking, "what is this person really about?"

We may "look into our bag" with disappointed eyes, seeing only a disjointed collection of odd objects: some depreciating currency, or some sentimental knickknacks whose weight has grown cumbersome, or cheap tricks, or a collection of masks, or even the hidden evidence of personal crimes. But whatever we see when we look into our bag, we are likely to find that *we do carry some skills*—even if presently unsharpened.

But most happy is the Individual whose natural crafty inventiveness does not bother itself much with what seems to be lacking from their bag. It's from this Individual's innate resourcefulness that they will devise, from whatever means they have at their disposal, the requirements for overcoming the challenges they're presently facing in this phase of life.

Whatever the Individual thinks they see, or however they perceive the value of the objects, gifts, skills, resources or personal characteristics they possess at present, the conclusion remains that we only have what we really have in any given moment, and those things which we truly and absolutely do have are things which originate from within and emerge from our own SELF.

Weapons and Tools

It's from these inner resources, no matter how great or how small they may currently seem, that the Initiate must forge the weapons of a warrior and the tools of an artist.

Your inner resources are now to be honed and sharpened. If you only have what you have, then you must put to good order your gifts and *understand your limitations* to survive the test of life's epic journey. It's through the discovery of inner resources and their efficient application to life's circumstances that the Initiate succeeds.

Be the Source of Your Own Resource

Dreams are given life directly through the SELF's pure desire. Willed completely and purely, the True Will shall someday inevitably trumpet its completion, and with its success shall come victory. The ultimate purpose of the Initiate's life will be accomplished.

Rising once again to the path, the Initiate takes aim at that distant Mountain. Moved forward by its subtle magnetism, the Individual progresses with a strange trust, no longer needing to know exactly where they're going or what they'll find.

As the path begins climbing upwards, every step becomes a willed affirmation of a future unknown. This phase is about discovery, not of knowing, but of coming to know.

A Search for the Kernel of Truth

The quest is now on the rise, yet the Mountain that looms has many shadowy crags and contours, some with steep drop-offs, precarious boulders and blind ways, and its whole landscape filled with the potential of things unknown. One may fear they'll find some terrible beast that's to greet them upon this lonely path; another may fear they'll find nothing at all!

Some who have sought the peak of this mountain have become lost in its shadows, some have exhausted themselves with sacrifice after sacrifice to what was just a false summit.

It's now in the very act of walking away from the past that the Individual clearly notices that they're gaining ground, both forward and upward. The exertion is increasing, but so is the view.

This opportunity to "really see something new" is enlightening, and with each step onward that something new is expanding. This is a good place to pause and take in the view.

Locate Yourself in the Greater Context of the Experience

From here, looking down the hill just climbed and out across the desert just traversed, your progress can already begin to be measured. On the horizon remains the last trace of those pillars of change that announced "The End," and simultaneously began the conscious birth of an unconscious idea whose contents are the genetics of the Initiate's very own being.

Looking down the hill it's plain to see that what has been accomplished so far is only a single step in a great climb. This challenge confirms that the Initiate possesses the inner strength to break the slavish chains of habit and to free the Mind from those restrictive impositions that do not truly exist. It's part of sovereign power itself to be able to be truly free.

For the Individual to do this they must free themselves from the constructs and preconceptions that have prevented them from apprehending who they truly are. This freedom is a prerequisite of conceiving the Seed-of-Self. Discovering it means honing down the veiled layers of the Individual's being, and resolving its complexity of ideas, concepts, and associations, layer by layer. Each simplification of those ideas removes a veil of complexity that has distorted and complicated the Individual's conception of their primordial Self.

The Seed-of-Self is the purified potential of your becoming. It's the simplest expression of Self. It's also a complete representation of Self, a totality not yet fully expressed—a sum of its inspired possibility. To reach it, the Individual must remove the "peel"—that rind of learned and accumulated reactions that have masked their true nature. To get at the truth of oneself it's necessary to pull back this outer layer enough to observe one's psycho-spiritual nakedness.

This involves the undressing of multiple masks of the True Self, identifying confused outer purposes of persona and getting beyond the interference of surface thoughts and utterances, deep, deep, deep into the core of Self where the light of purpose first ignited the spirit. There the Seed-of-Self resides with a message unique and transcendent, a fortune cookie held aloft for that Individual alone to crack open.

But before that is a veil of complexity with multiple layers and distortions from imprints made upon the psyche throughout its development. Some are the smudged, dirty fingerprints of educators, caretakers, and those trying to be helpful. Some layers are pure armor, made to protect. Some are complex webs cross-threaded with unconscious suggestions whose viral manipulations lie at such a deeply unconscious level that their menace is allowed to continue for years because their origin remains unknown.

The Seed-of-Self is the Individual's pure essence, the very elemental unit of Self. The Individual's interest, hobbies, abilities, goals, motivations, values, beliefs, and deepest drives can be possible clues to its essential character. But this requires that one be capable of being honest with oneself.

Most people are unconscious of the layers of self-deception they wrap themselves in. Often the very image a person thinks of as themselves is just a cloak to confuse and deceive others, a disguise to protect them and reduce vulnerability. If and when the Individual is deceived by the design of their own deception, a complex degeneration is given room to begin.

Small compromises in an Individual's authenticity continue growing until the Individual either gives way to greater personal betrayals or takes corrective action. The Individual who's being honest with themselves, even when they feel quite certain they've been true to their self can often be confronted with the realization that they have instead (sometimes for many years) been true to an "image of self" which was less their True Self and more of a self-deception. The Individual must ask until they are certain beyond a reasonable doubt, "Is this my True Self? Or is it just a flattering misconception of who I have mistakenly fancied myself to be?

Once you discover this seed and hold it in your hand you must figure out what it needs. How will you cultivate it? Acknowledging what's the True Self, and rejecting all else, allows for the power of focus, and it's much easier to focus on that which is simple.

One of the consequences of this focus is freedom from those concerns, entanglements, and impediments of the outside world that hem-in the development of most ordinary people. The complexity of the world seeks to infect the Individual with its fatal aimlessness and lack of coherent unity. It's in the belief of psychologist Carl Jung that contact with society corrupts the connection with True Self. Hence, a period of separation is required to fertilize the process. This is the key role and ultimate purpose of lengthy meditation during initiation. It involves setting apart a time and place for its processes to unravel, a world apart where the Seed-of-Self can conceal the mysteries of its germination from the profane.

Discovering True Will means eliminating all irrelevant desires and choosing instead to hone down on the most important facts and arrange them into a coherent understanding like pieces of a puzzle. Each piece of the puzzle is a symbol of something, and vice versa. The curious arrangement of these emerging symbols forms an image of the Secret Self. It's in the language of these personal symbols that a person and their inner being communicate.

Seemingly from another mind, comes that mystical voice who announces a mythic dimension that lies beyond. It makes itself known as an elemental force of consciousness, hinting at its Identity flirtatiously through the symbols of the Mind. The Initiate must pick out the original thread from Gordian's Knot, before they draw their sword. Like Alexander they might ask themselves, "Which of my emerging impulses lack any apparent calculation?" What is original must, of necessity, also be unpredictable.

The force of True Will seeks to express its elemental nature in certain words, ideas, symbols, feelings, thoughts, stories, preferences, interests, innate tendencies, abilities, drives, dreams, and so on. In this way, the Seed-of-Self is constantly seeking to express its natural vigor and tendencies.

Without identifying the authentic nature of True Will it's impossible to cultivate it. For this reason, it's highly likely that its existence is being blatantly overlooked, or hidden in plain sight, if only for the simple fact that it may initially appear underdeveloped when compared with the invasive will-force of the Phantom Self. Likewise, some people purposely choose (under much strain) to hedge the development of their True Will simply because it clashes with the persona they have fabricated for use as a social mask.

It's these les Miserables whose True Will is constantly being overshadowed by the rapid growth of thorny weeds whose seed was sown by the mindless mischief of the Phantom Self.

THE SEED-OF-SELF:

In the next phase, you'll discover those components that have sought to express the nature and Will of the Hidden Self. Think of this phase as mining after material and arranging it for the purposes of identifying its underlying meaning. It's here that the magic happens.

Discovering the Seed-of-Self

First, begin unmasking the outer layers of "ought to" and begin refining and simplifying what you want. Then move progressively layer by layer deeper into that question seeking to find the place beyond what you "just want" and into the deeper layers of *what you Will.*

This process can generate a fair amount of information about the surface structure of the Mind. The answers that come up most naturally are the ones to go with. In the act of delving into their Core, the Individual is seeking to behold a sort of symbolic naked revealing of their deepest motivations and beliefs regarding their life's purpose. The challenge here is one of courage, of stark bravery.

"If you bring forth what is within you, what you bring forth will save you. If you do not bring forth what is within you, what you do not bring forth will destroy you."

-The Gospel of Thomas

For this challenge, victory is twofold.

First, you must be able to behold the naked truth of yourself, stripped of defenses, excuses, accusations, reasonings, and self-deluding fabrications.

Second, you must acknowledge the reality of the truth you find, and accept the challenges that stand between where you are and where you want to be. You must not only accept this truth, but also affirm it, must not only affirm it but *come to love it* as the purest and noblest expression of SELF, as the ever-incarnating life of your divine WILL.

Every honeybee instinctively knows its True Will is an echo of Universal Will, a divine instinct whose motion mirrors the motion of the cosmos. Otherwise, it's beyond comprehension that bees would give themselves over to their Will and to their Work with so little hesitation or lateral concern for the possible effects of their actions. Does the bee even know that it's greedy pursuit of life's nectar is instrumental in an uncountable number of nature's essential processes? We can scarcely imagine that a bee really understands the vital importance of its selfish obsession with robbing flowers of their sweet substance. If it did understand it would probably be too much responsibility for any creature to bear. Instead nature just says, "Live your Will." The bee obliges by following its ultimate self-interest and miraculously, the world is saved.

Understanding this, the activated True Will of the Individual becomes the highest expression of human divinity—the incarnation of Universal Will.

Life as Art

To step upon this sublime path of True Will is to become the author of one's own life. With creative pen and brush in hand, the Initiate beholds in themselves the possibility—the potential—of completing the statement:

"The thing that I truly know that I must be and do is (insert drum-roll):

_____."

CHALLENGE:

Application for Initiation

Know the Seed -of- Thyself

Basic concept: The Seed-of-Self embodies your true essence, nature, and objective. Get to "Know Thyself," the original Self where the power truly is. It represents the gold-of-who-you-are and shall contribute the raw materials for your mythic story.

Image: a golden seed inside a labyrinth of concentric spiral rings waiting to be unraveled so that it can take root.

Challenge: Begin moving through the layers of conditioning and developmental imprints that have left their smudged fingerprints on your authentic being.

Actions to take: Rid yourself of the constructs and preconceptions that have made it difficult for you to apprehend who you truly are. Go beyond the mind's surface thoughts and utterances, past the multiple masks of the persona, through the veiled layers of the mind and discover the Seed-of-Self. Simplify the veil of complexity that hides the true self. Simplicity is the self's purity.

Hang up the cloak of artificiality—that hastily constructed garment that has shamefully served to cover the nakedness of your original being.

Concentrate your forces on what you actually are, and rid yourself of the misrepresenting misconceptions, personal propaganda and sly social masks that contrive to paint a false picture of who you only fancy yourself to be.

It's quite possible that through this process you may become aware of how, for most people, the Seed-of-Self becomes wrapped in layers of lies that act as distortions and filters of the original impulses and light of the True Self.

The goal of this phase is to develop true self-awareness, and align yourself with your essential nature. Resolve yourself from the complex to the simple, clarify your essence from the vague to the clear.

Express your simplicity: Write down twenty-four words that you associate with yourself. Then begin marking them out until you're left with only one, the one that best and most simply expresses your Self.

For greater depth, analyze your skills, hobbies, passions, drives, goals, motivations, beliefs, interests, and values for the thread of connection that weaves them all together. Ask yourself honestly, what is working below the surface that connects all the various elements of your life? Bullshit aside, what are you really up to?

Getting to know your Core reflects the ancient advice carved above the oracle at Delphi to "Know Thyself." Understanding your Core means that you know what you value, and what you Will. First, practice being brutally honest with yourself. Then righteously affirm and accept your emerging inner truth.

To begin discovering your core values, ask yourself these three questions (I learned these when becoming a Master Practitioner of Neuro-Linguistic Programming):

(1.) What do I need to have in my life right now to feel like it's worth living? _____

_____

(2.) When you get your answer ask, "What does that allow me to do, or experience?" _____

_____

(3.) As you imagine that, what feeling does it give you? _____
_____ (your Core Value)

As you come to understand yourself more deeply, you will gain insight and clarity into your subconscious driver (what psychologists call your Natural Lead Function). Decipher the connections between your interests, abilities, and deeply held values for clues about the Core of who you are and what you represent.

Knowing your inner components helps you understand and formulate a grand vision for your life. Understanding your grand vision gives you a mission and a mission allows you to develop and employ far-seeing strategies. Having a mission means that what you do is motivated by a deeply rewarding sense-of-purpose. This comes from living in alignment with your core values, i.e. cultivating your Seed-of-Self.

A Bit of Science

The psychologist Carl Jung calls the process of becoming whole the process of Individuation. Essentially, it's the process of the Individual becoming what they always were—in potential. He went on to suggest that what interferes with this process of becoming whole is contamination from society. It's through socialization that we can be led astray.

The healthiest form of life, psychologically speaking, would be one where the Individual can live and act in accordance with True Self. In this veritable Eden, circumstances would be supporting what psychologists call "the Natural Lead Function," a place where the Individual is using their innate giftedness within an environment that both rewards and supports it. In this place, the natural self and its original impulse (it's believed) would be moved exclusively by the proper guiding force, True Will.

What has made this so difficult within the bounds of society is another thing that psychologists have named, "consensus trance."

Consensus Trance: A state of automated consciousness or mass hypnosis in which the beliefs that a person holds are generated by others rather than from the experience of realizing those truths for themselves.

In this way, a person loses themselves to various currents of mainstream thought. Even "alternative thought" carries the heavy burden of consensus liability, and much like the mainstream thought that it opposes, will aggressively pursue the social shaming of those Individuals who inadvertently show signs of having broken with its collective trance to trod more original paths. To truly have original thoughts in our present age is almost a sure sign of genius in some form or another.

The problem that perpetuates itself in the person who cannot seem to hear their original thoughts amongst the mass clamoring of a hypnotized society is the slippery slope known by psychologists as Falsification of Type.

Falsification of Type: A compulsion to act in a way contrary to one's nature.

How does the falsification of type work? How does it progress?

First, a person learns to adapt themselves to circumstances outside their natural inclinations (True Will). This sounds good. It's a natural part of life to adapt, right? Yes, but...the slippery slope!

Second, a person learns to compromise. This often manifests as a sort of social training disguised as an education. It's this "another brick in the wall" style education that cleverly repackages its anthem so that it's curtailed to prevailing generational myths while retaining its central lecture of consensus obligation. It aims to redirect the Individual's innate truth into a modified configuration of popular consensus.

So often, the concentrated essence of this "education" is to constrain the Individual into doing what's ultimately in conflict with their deep-seated instincts and incongruent with their most natural inclinations (True Will).

This contrived consensus achieves its desired effect through a dual strategy, attacking from two different angles. For the Individual who dares to break with popular consensus there are the insinuated threats of social shaming, sexual rejection, and perhaps even a ruined career. On the other hand, for those who consent, the future is allegedly full of promise. Advertising professionals captivate their audience with animated allusions of fulfillment, endless fantasies (financial success, popularity, and sex) awaiting those who willingly conform their self-expression to sanctioned brands.

The problem for so many people is that the hook of consensus is baited with what seems like sound logic. It begins simply enough, and at a tender age. We are all taught the need to compromise in kinder-garten as part of the socialization process. The problem, however, soon emerges with the difficulty of setting boundaries for these outwardly imposed compromises.

Ever more aggressively we are demanded to submit our rights as Individuals to the "interest of the group." More and more the Individual is expected to bow to an ever diversifying and conflicted assortment of communal interest labeled as "the good of society." Shamelessly, unnamed agendas are furthered at the expense of Individual liberty.

In progressive fashion, the Individual is yoked with political correctness, bound to serve an ever-growing assortment of foreign social contracts. With utter moral righteousness Individual liberty is fettered by casual references to a vague mystical heaven called "equality." In this social Nirvana technology becomes little more than a medium through which to streamline collective consciousness to the cost-effec-tive contours of contemporary social agendas.

Because of this shameless manipulation, a most serious question arises—when do we finally recognize that we've made an unhealthy habit of compromising our values, our beliefs, and ultimately our Sovereignty as Individuals to the demiurge of the New World—Consensus?

The march of progress advances along the icy rutted cliffs of Individual compromise.

Once again the slippery slope, but in this case, it becomes an increas-ingly dangerous slip as it ultimately moves us closer to the precipice of what could very likely be a fatal fall.

The third and final step of degeneration known as the Falsification of Type is when a person who has learned to adapt and compromise themselves, at last, learns to betray themselves—for money, for fame, for accreditation, or for fear of social shaming. It is here that many lose themselves to herd mentality and become just another face in a crowd of mass-minded pseudo-individuals caught in a trending current of popular "opinion."

For the Sovereign Individual, this is dangerous ground, for it's this descent from True Will to falsification that robs a person of their Crown. If this goes on long enough the person afflicted with separation from their True Will can develop a psychologically nasty condition with all sorts of health-related problems from impotence, to premature aging, to cancer and death. This condition is called "Prolonged Adaptive Stress Disorder," which is a stress-related disorder that is perpetuated when a person is forced, by external circumstances, to live outside their natural inclinations.

Something Mystical

The religion of Thelema teaches that each person is to seek his or her own divine will. In its mystical text, called The Book of the Law, is written, "Do what thou wilt is the whole of the law," meaning that the cosmic law, universal law (not human law), calls for the Individual to live by the code of their own TRUE WILL.

It goes even further to suggest that as a reflection of cosmic law, one's inner law must be obeyed. The Book of the Law states, "Thou hast no right but to do thy will." The central commandment of this spiritual text is for the Initiate to take up this cosmic law as their own.

Prophets are those Individuals who have a unique and personal experience with the divine, and often their lives will topple the existing (though no doubt decaying) order. Those who follow the letter of a law that they did not personally receive, but rather, are following a book or a prescribed text are not prophets, but saints. Saints obey the laws of others, that's what they're good at. Prophets obey the laws they receive themselves. One is the source of divinity, the other a mere scribe. The Sovereign Individual is a prophet of their own law.

There's no power higher than the Individual who has attained the Sovereign state. By definition, a Sovereign is an authority unto themselves: absolute, supreme, and with unlimited power in their realm (here the "realm" begins with the Individual's own consciousness).

The Sovereign Individual who claims their divine right is the source of their own spiritual law. There's no other earthly power higher than the Sovereign Individual; there's no other who can issue commands to them. The Sovereign is hence the source of this spiritual law—the Law of True Will. This is a mighty place to be in.

My Experience

I've watched my children running around for hours playing with what seemed like unlimited energy and enthusiasm until I ask if they could help pick up the mess they've been creating. That's when their shoulders slump and they become overcome with lethargy. They can barely summon the energy to reach down and pick up a crayon.

That's the difference between True Will and an enforced will. One study suggested that it takes one-hundred times more energy to do something you don't want to do in comparison to something that you want to do. It requires more oxygen as it taxes the Individual's entire system. On the other hand, it takes no discipline to do what you want to do, it feels effortless (unless you've been trained otherwise).

Many times, I've felt this with jobs I didn't like, with events I didn't want to attend, with people I didn't want to see. Yet, while I was avoiding those things I happily toiled away at my self-chosen occupations, whatever they were at the time: books, spontaneous art projects, physical exercise, rituals etc.

However, it's very challenging to do one's True Will and nothing else. It takes awareness, commitment, and the unique skill of saying no to all that does not fall under the jurisdiction of True Will.

It's a Master indeed who can succeed in, what might seem at times to be a puritanical pursuit. Yet, that is what this spiritual law calls us to do, to stay on the path of True Will and not to stray lest we find ourselves committing the three progressive sins of falsification: to adapt, to compromise, and to betray.

"[T]here is verily either a Divine Right or else a Diabolic Wrong; one or the other of these two."

-Thomas Carlye, On Heroes

There have been many times when I've adapted my beliefs to take the shape of present company. It just seemed easier. To preserve struggling relationships, I compromised my values and censored myself, but in time the relationships still died. It was then I found myself truly alone and far from my path. The times that I betrayed myself can still be counted by the raised scars left by such stupidity. They now serve as reminders of the wages of sin.

LAPIS EXILIS

INITIATION

CHAPTER FOUR

Cultivate a Mythic Story

"...only a horizon ringed about with myths can unify a culture."

-Nietzsche

What the Individual attaches to "I AM," in turn attaches itself to the Individual. "I AM" is built of relationships: with thoughts, with feelings, with ideas, and yes with people, with status, with money, with education and on and on.

Individuals build their Self-Concept through associations. People may magnetically resonate with some idea, or even some color, or number. Subconsciously these symbols form and express our mind's pre-literal reality. With the help of the Initiate's own artistic arrangement, these strange symbols begin to take on the shape of a collage revealing a hidden image.

This emerging image may be seen as a unity of parts, as if you've caught a glimpse of the axle which secretly governs the various forces of your being. In this archetypal representation you'll find an image symbolic of the whole of your consciousness. This evolving symbol is the talisman of a new inner life, the holy sigil of Individual consciousness. It is in this creation that the hidden nature of "I AM" expresses itself to the conscious mind.

The Seed-of-Self phase is best approached as an artist might. The objective is to intelligently and aesthetically arrange a collection of hieroglyphic images in a way that can "spell" an underlying idea. As the Initiate begins to use interpretation of this idea as a sort of ongoing meditation, the force which this image conveys gradually begins to make itself known to consciousness, at the same time revealing itself as the seed of something that is both surprisingly original and yet as indigenous to the Individual's character as electricity is to Earth.

It's this symbolic idea whose existence represents the underlying hidden force which connects them. The Seed-of-Self is like the genetic material of a thing-to-be, a thing that's becoming, and the "I AM" is the sprout that is emerging from the top of that seed. It's this symbol which represents the Seed-of-Self's first urge to life, that stage when it still tenderly holds to its pure ideal. To a nation, this is its flag.

Old-Limiting Story

Old-Limiting Stories are chronological stories defined by events locked in the past, and often recited within the emotional context of concretized reactions to "remembered" events. In essence, they are tales of the dead.

Referencing the storyline of yesterday to make decisions for today is the same as using an out-of-date map. Locked to previous storylines and divorced from creative potential, the Old-Limiting Story lacks the imaginative power of self-creation.

Old Limiting stories fill the history books, but the real story of "I AM" is much more than a chronological recitation of physical events because those old-limiting stories do not account for the presence of evolving forces *within* the Individual.

Self-Creation, on the other hand, bears none of those heavy chronological chains. What would otherwise be chains becomes many chiming bells and trinkets attached to the arms and legs of some great, multi-armed Hindu-god—crushing entire worlds as he dances, and giving birth to new ones from his forehead.

This God grants his chosen few a unique freedom based on a law much higher than established reason. This God understands that "editing" is a necessary (and sacred) corrective adjunct to the wild, inherent dynamism of evolving consciousness. Ruthlessly this God weeds his garden.

This particular freedom grants the Initiate the ability to crush old worlds and to create new ones. They get to discover for themselves what kind of monsters they might become if they were to wield the power of a God.

This power requires something to give it form, to activate it. This will be our proverbial Ark of the Covenant. With this Ark we will demonstrate our new power, carrying it before us like a holy relic upon which a whole new epoch will be established. We will call this Ark "The New Constructive Myth."

"Myth is an image or representation which points to something essentially unknown, a mystery."

-Edward Edinger, Ego and Archetype

Your New Constructive Myth

The power of a New Constructive Myth is that it enables the Individual to create themselves within the medium of an artistic-magical psychology. Constructing a New Myth requires both the freedom of the artist and the forethought of the entrepreneur. A person doing their banking with an Old-Limiting story is only reacting, time and time again, to ideas and actions stamped by the authority of a book that is no longer being actively written.

The true value of perception resides in how recently it has been updated, reconsidered and readjusted. Realizing this, a genius of military strategy developed the OODA loop. Observe, Orient, Decide, Act. Then repeat as conditions are changing.

It has been suggested that even in their most exalted moods, humans are incapable of truth. The truth of this statement we, of course, do not know. The important point is that even under the best conditions it's nearly impossible to know the truth of something, whether it already happened or is currently happening. This might be for no better reason than the act of observing a thing changes it. If an Individual can only know something by observing it, then they must also be changing it, and so to know something is also to change it.

The more an Individual knows about themselves, the more that knowledge comes under the influence of their Will. The more it does, the greater will be their innate and natural tendency to continue shaping it. If a person or a history book began changing their chronological story it would likely arouse suspicion as to their intentions. In essence, such changes would constitute a form of lying. Yet, the shaping and changing of oneself with a New Constructive Myth is a craft, an artistic work, a bold new truth chiseled from the stubborn granite of historic assumptions.

Constructing a New Myth is an art whose medium is the psyche. It's the psyche, like Pharaoh, who takes command of the pen and the brush of self-creation—a reality both chosen and cultivated. The Initiate is artistically becoming the source of their own story.

The purpose of this evolving myth is to define the deeper meaning of the Individual's existence. The process of its creation will teach them to communicate with their Higher Self—a mythical being who thinks and communicates in mythical patterns. The construction of this New Myth is part of the overall ritual process of redefining the Individual's relationship to life.

The Seed-of-Self is symbolically sprouting the reputation the Individual is growing into. It initiates a change in the relationship to the person that the Individual used to be.

Before this, they were letting history dictate the future, and a large part of that history's origin exists in the upbringing that established their identity.

In the vulnerable state of infancy, the Individual receives a name, symbolically being defined by someone else. This is the root of the unconscious process of self-creation.

Unless the Individual has been thoughtfully and intelligently groomed (without error) from birth, then they may well consider taking a creative look at the foundational processes of their psyche. A new Constructive Myth begins with clearing away the debris of chronological contents and proceeds with laying the foundations of something truly great.

This new constructive myth begins with the creation of a symbolic representation of the beliefs that will characterize the new you. This representation is composed of an arrangement of symbolic ideas that adequately expresses the force of the Individual's "I AM" and via the subconscious mind, puts it into motion.

The Mythic Story is a deeper, more significant, more resourceful truth that lies behind the Old-Limiting Story. To command the pen of self-creation is to command the sword of authority over one's being. By becoming the scriptwriter for one's destiny, the Individual becomes an "Author" and thus also an "Authority" in their own right, in their own life.

This "right" is the right to write, to carve for oneself. It's a person's inherent right to create themselves and their experience. No longer must they allow themselves to be defined by what lies outside of them or allow it to influence their story. No longer will "I AM" be communal property.

In any given story there is both the content and the meaning behind the content. There is the surface structure happening and there is a deeper structure operating. Always, there is the seen and the unseen, the apparent and the not so apparent.

It's not the changing of "facts" that brings the Individual power as much as it is the ability to command a poetic and inspired interpretation of those "facts." It's the artistic ability to formulate a meaning that transcends those facts.

The Key to the Imagination

The Individual's Constructive Myth represents a new and vital belief hewed from the Individual's life themes. The story that an Individual is telling themselves about themselves acts as unconscious programming and plays an important part in manifesting the "reality" that the Individual experiences.

In the imagination, belief is the key that sets formation free. It's a key called "belief" and it opens the door to shape reality. To believe means "to make real."

The Flag of the Sovereign Self

The object in this phase is to create a symbol, mandala or primordial image to communicate the Individual's evolving identity via myth to the unconscious mind in a language that it understands. To do this effectively it's necessary for the Individual to craft a myth and bring it to life using symbol and metaphor.

Stories will always contain an element of fiction, a distortion born from perspective. Some facts will be neglected, others will be overly emphasized, it's the nature of storytelling. A self-constructed myth takes this fact and turns it into an art, intentionally crafting a symbolic story that serves the purposes of consciousness. The use of myth and symbol exhilarates the hidden roots of motivation within consciousness. By communicating in a language beyond reason, the mind moves beyond the limits of reason and into the world of formation existing in the unconscious regions of the mind.

The Strongest Story Wins

The mythic story is the creation of one's life. The power to create and tell one's own story is the power of choice. Every choice made by an Individual reflects a deeper set of beliefs and values that are embedded in the subconscious mythology they're living out.

Being the Author of one's own life means developing a strong sense of one's origin. It means cultivating a distinct point of view and recognizing where upbringing and the existing culture has made a decided contribution. Established internal mythologies are reflected in the surface structure of internal dialogue and the mind's superficial thoughts and utterances. A person's inner world sits upon a deeper understructure. It hangs on the rhythms of a subconscious Myth.

Commanding a New Constructive Myth means taking it by the leash and leading it.

That leash is the "Universal Theme" behind the Myth and the collar is the core value or aspiration that connects the Individual with the Myth. Instead of drowning in chronological contents, what you want is clarity on the purpose for which your New Constructive Myth is being created.

The Illustrious Purpose: to Formulate a Myth

Myth is formulated in a place of extended possibility whose magical border is conterminous with one's unconscious mind. Individuals are measured by their stories. Growth requires that the Individual's thinking, identity, and consciousness adapt in a survival of the fittest fashion. The strongest story wins.

After the formulation of an epic, heroic Myth, the only question that remains to be answered is how will the Individual model or demonstrate that New Constructive Myth in their daily actions?

CHALLENGE:

Application for Self-Initiation

Cultivate a Mythic Story

Basic Concept: The True Nature of your Spirit runs deeper than words can describe. That's why creating a symbol or metaphor can greatly enhance your power by enabling your conscious mind to speak to the unconscious mind in a language it understands. This symbol will act as a bridge between those two minds, completing the creative circuit and sparking your latent genius.

Image: The Flag of your Sovereign Self sprouting from the Seed-of-Self, a figurative design of your "I AM."

Objective: Take a mythic stance toward your own life. Create a symbol, mandala, or primordial image to communicate intention and Identity (myth) to the unconscious mind (a mythical being that thinks in mythical patterns) in a language it understands. The symbol you are developing is a mnemonic device and a bridge that maintains the flow of instinctive energies from the unconscious to the conscious mind.

Through this Flag of your Sovereign Self, its image and attending mythology, you are learning to become the Author (creative authority) of your own life, beginning by generating a Mythic Story. This mythic story is the deeper, more significant, more resourceful truth that lies behind the old-limited story. The creation of its corresponding image will allow you to artistically synchronize your vision with the unconscious force of your emerging True Will.

Step One: Ask yourself if you have an old-limiting story about who you are, one that is based on who you were. If so, consider the value of editing this story, even rewriting it with some added flare. We will refer to this as a New Constructive Myth. It's the story of you becoming who you have the potential to be.

Action to take: To begin creating your new constructive myth, choose the universal theme for your life, one that reflects your deeper set of beliefs and values. Become the scriptwriter for destiny by taking creative control of the story you've been telling yourself about who you are. To do this, reframe your experiences so that they reflect your renewed relationship to life. As Nietzsche said, "There are no facts, only interpretations." Feel free to loosen the bonds of fact, those narratives by which you have been fettered, as you artfully mold your story into a reflection of your Highest Ideal.

Step Two: Your symbol will act as your brand, and as a reminder of the reputation you are growing into. As you consider it, think symbolically. What colors, ideas or images represent your evolving conception of Self?

Action to take: Create a symbol that defines your deeper nature. If it helps, imagine that you are designing a flag that represents you and your cause. When this symbol causes you to feel a deep sense of personal resonance, you've succeeded. As you synchronize yourself with your symbol, enjoy the new feelings that emerge.

A Bit of Science

Hypnotherapists know that a person's "story" unconsciously manifest their reality. Science sometimes refers to a "morphogenic field," like an aura that is generated from a person's unconscious beliefs and has the power to affect plants, fungi, electronics, and other people. It hints at a mysterious capacity for a person's internal thoughts and beliefs to radiate into the world and cause things to happen. This is one way that the law of attraction may be explained.

Nathaniel Branden, the author of the Six-Pillars of Self-Esteem said that "Self-concept is destiny." Essentially, what a person comes to believe about themselves unconsciously shapes, and, to a point, determines their destiny.

By creating a New Constructive Myth, a person is becoming the scriptwriter for destiny, laying the foundation of something great. Constructing your myth means defining your new relationship to life and changing the relationship to the person you used to be. It means no longer letting someone else define you or letting history dictate the future. It means being the source of your own Story.

It's one thing to know something consciously and it's another thing to completely incorporate (and apply) that knowledge at a deep, unconscious level so that it manifests itself effortlessly. That's the ultimate mastery, and when it comes to our True Nature, we want it to manifest effortlessly and without our having to think about it.

Something Mystical

The power of symbols and talismans forms a large bulk of occult wisdom. Ancient cultures filled their everyday lives with reminders of the hidden forces of nature. Symbolic representations of man-made forces can become potent reminders of living energies, and as such allow those forces to be invoked into consciousness. Examples of such symbolic representations are the standard carried before the legions of Rome, the pentagram of witchcraft, the family crest of medieval Europe and even the American flag today. They are all symbolic representations of the spirit of certain ideas.

In the practice of ceremonial magic, one of the preparatory tasks of the magician is to create a "lamen," a talisman worn over the heart with a symbol of the spirit that one wishes to invoke.

In the case of our work here, the spirit that we wish to invoke is that of our True Will, and hence the symbol that we create for our purpose will be one that accurately represents it and actualizes it in symbolic form.

My Experience

At the start of my initiation I had the story of all stories, the problem was that it concluded upon a rather tragic note. When I began crafting a New Constructive Myth this at first posed a problem. It's not that we begin to tell ourselves lies when myth-making, it's that we begin to see the skewed perceptions inherent in our old-limiting stories and learn to reframe our experience in alignment with the truth of a new understanding.

It's said that the Pharaohs only immortalized their successes. They've been criticized for this by those who have naturally felt inferior. At the same time, historians have found evidence to suggest that even the Torah and Bible are essentially less factual than mythic, containing triumphs and events collected from many different ancient cultures. Yet those writings have persisted through centuries and served a purpose— that of creating vital myths that have been used to both nourish and legitimize the worldview of the cultures who created them. Power in the making! Proof that factual accuracy is not a requirement of mystical truth—perpetual insistence is!

From the wisdom of the Pharaoh, we can learn to avoid carving perceived failures in stone. Highlight what makes you great. Use what's useful and discard all the rest.

Many times throughout life, I've watched what seemed to be a mistake put me on a new and brighter path. I've more than once regretted an action, only to look back on that action years later and see how necessary it was. The more experience I have, the more I see that all experience has some value from which wisdom might be gained.

Looking at things in a new way helps us to reframe them. Many experiences can be recycled to new uses. When creating your New Constructive Myth, identify your life-themes and craft them into an epic storyline with room to grow. When creating your symbol go deep; resurrect early childhood feelings and emotions of awe and grandeur. Let the enthusiasm of the divine child sketch its outline. Once you have this image, look upon it often as a reminder. It can become a piece of art or turned into symbol to be worn around the neck.

After I created my symbol, I had it cast in pure gold. Remember that this symbol represents your True Will, your life purpose and your Mythic Self, hence its representation is sacred.

LAPIS EXILIS

INITIATION

CHAPTER FIVE

Construct a Ritual of Inevitablility

> "Anytime you have Individuation occurring, you
> also have ritualization occurring."
>
> -Robert L. Moore, The Archetype of Initiation

Constructing a Ritual of Inevitability begins with the Individual asking the question, "How will I get what I want with what I have?"

Having probed their depths to divine the deeper meaning and life-purpose behind their "I AM" statement, the Individual next develops their Evolving Ability Potential. This is closely related to the Natural Lead Function spoken of by psychologists. It represents some particular gift, innate motivation or natural leading tendency that the Individual possesses. This natural gift is in their "Nature," and often functions effortlessly because (in psychological terms) it's supported by the attitude that corresponds to the Individual's natural type.

Having come to "Know ThySelf," it's possible to align one's actions with the deepest purpose of their "I AM." This is a Ritual set in motion by the Initiate's own hands. It's a ritual of cultivating one's "I AM" concept, tending it from that tender seed, cultivating it until it roots, grows, and blooms; keeping to the task as the idea is made into the real.

To Be... Do!

The Ritual of Inevitability is the starting place from which a revolution is set in motion. It will gradually transform the Individual's entire world into a reflection of their deepest aspirations. In time, the Ritual accumulates a momentum of its own, a life of its own, a heartbeat of its own.

More and more effortlessly, it seems, actions are now matching intent.

A generative process of acceleration compels the Individual's natural giftedness to develop its skills. As this power grows, tasks are mastered. The challenges required by the newly emerging values are met, setting in motion a pattern of success as a result of work manifested in the realm of personal genius. It's here that one's values and highest intention compel excellence.

The "I AM" commands the inevitability of its aim by the rooted purity of its aspiration and the sheer momentum of "the Rituals" repetition.

The Rituals

Ritual represents the active part of a commitment. Coming to understand the commitments inherent in one's True Will, the Individual now seeks to demonstrate intent in action, while at the same time cultivating those latent powers that will be necessary to fulfill those commitments.

They ask themselves frankly, "How will I demonstrate the Godhood of my Nature?"

Yet more practically speaking, the question becomes, "How do I convert the identity of my immortal "I AM" into actions?"

For some, moving through these turn-styles of greatness will mean going from the phase of being an intellectual thinker, into a passionate doer. The persistence of a daily ritual builds a momentum of inevitability that is an outgrowth of commitment. Designing the day like a ritual, staying on target, tending your flock, minding your business, cultivating your crop—are symbolic of this ritual whose aim is to produce momentum. Gradually, actions become echoes of "I AM." In time all thoughts, words, and deeds become congruent with one's sole purpose.

This phase of initiation is about skill development, committing to certain gifts and honing them. This is the cultivation phase of the Seed-of-Self. After the pattern break of New Neurology, the mind is in the best position to learn. The frontal lobes are activated and the freewill decision-making function may now be focused to transform thinking into being.

Commit to Your Gift

In discovering this gift, in identifying it, remember that potency is potential. Ask yourself, "Where am I the most potent?" Consider that if you're not good at something, it's because you've been designed to be great at something else. A wine opener makes a poor knife.

The lesson of this phase is about committing to your work and remaining within your circle of commitment. The key to power is commitment. Commit to your Gift.

The challenge is to consistently perform these generative life rituals, to continuously advance the development of one's Evolving Ability Potential.

I WANT it, but do I WILL it?

Often, there is a contest between what a person "wants" and what they "Will."

For example, imagine that a person's "Will" is to become the greatest boxer of all time, but they "want" to eat chocolate cake and drink tequila at night. In such a case, what they want is incongruent with what they Will. For the Sovereign Individual, Will is superior to want.

The Myth Sets the Tone of the Ritual.

The Ritual is the momentum of the Myth. You might even say that it's "the Spirit" of the Myth. During this phase, you're establishing a daily routine of power. The purpose of this routine is to develop the resources and skills required to master the challenges that stand between you and what you ultimately value. It's here and now that the Initiate learns to use what's in their bag.

The commitment to Self must become a commitment expressed in actions.

The Ritual is the Motion of the Myth.

The ritual acts as a method for strengthening the habit of Will; it's the development of the gravity of habit that furthers the Will. Previously, the Initiate learned to use and strengthen their Will by over-coming unconscious habits while developing New Neurology. Now, their strengthened Will is applied to the establishment of new habits. It's these new habits whose accumulated momentum will lead to the inevitability of the desired outcome. The motion of the Ritual is, like the King roaring forth in his chariot—an idea in motion.

Cultivating the Seed-of-Self

The Ritual of cultivating the Seed-of-Self is accomplished with the Will, a form of energized enthusiasm. It affirms the very being of the "I AM"—manifesting its force in the repetition of highly significant actions that represent the life of the Will. Cultivating the Seed-of-Self through the Ritual of Inevitability forms the very heart of the process of Self-Creation, and hence its performance is sacred to the Individual.

It's through this Ritual that the Individual exercises their gifts, and gradually ascends upward with compiled efforts onto a platform of Mastery. It's from here that the Individual can begin to reign over conditions and circumstances. All that lies between the Individual and their aims must, in time, be encountered and conquered. This means one must know beyond a shadow of a doubt that the strength of their "I AM" is equal to or greater than all that it will meet.

LAPIS EXILIS

Know the jurisdiction of your power,
your Kingdom,
the circle of your real concern,
so that you may concentrate,
all of your energies,
upon the Ritual,
of tending its bloom
unto completion.

Fueled by Will's persuasive force the wheels of the Ritual turn, carrying the Campaign ever onward and closer toward the destined completion of the "Great Work."

It's to this great end that Kings do tend; their work building a firm base from which to ascend unto a final capstone. This capstone surmounts the Pharaoh's monument and marks the completion of the oath to True Will.

Its completion is the Great Work, the Individual's symbolic pyramid.

The Great Work is a monument to effort, built of a staggering number of individual blocks. Its completion represents the accumulated evidence of a Will, a mountain made of the work of an entire lifetime. Fully committed to this awesome task, the Individual's entire being collaborates in a unitive Ritual of Inevitability, laboring in both the light and the shadow of its mounting product—a work of pure love, masterfully completed as the ultimate gift, both to the Self and to the World—the enduring work of an "Immortal Legacy."

These are the terms and conditions the would-be King sets out to conquer.

The Middle Gate

The Middle Gate represents a specific point of attainment, it's the gateway of propulsion. It's the point of the journey marked by a reversal of gravity—it's the experience of moving from friction to forward momentum. Up until the Middle Gate, the Individual was exerting themselves against themselves, against the mass of their own inertia. The resistance that seemed so monumental at the beginning of the journey and was at the root of the Individual's problems, is now converted from drag into g-force.

The earlier feelings of restlessness, impatience, dissatisfaction, and yearning are now being replaced by the single-minded rotation of the Mind around the Ritual. The rhythm of one's efforts now have a hypnotic effect. The Individual finds themselves being entranced by their steady repetition, gathering more and more momentum, as one continues the Ritual of Inevitability. The path and the goal are becoming one.

Success in this phase is a result of maintaining creative control of one's willed Identity and using it both as a source of guidance and power. Self-belief becomes the gravity of the Individual's internal Sun. This, in turn, becomes both their guiding star and the seat of their Throne. Love for the Great Work becomes its own reward, and the momentum of that work is growing.

Love for the Great Work

Essential to sustaining one's efforts is a heartfelt love for the work being chosen. When what we do comes from this place, it's possible to tap into a seemingly inexhaustible well of energy that allows our gifts to manifest naturally and to develop a momentum that can, at times, move the Will forth almost effortlessly. This energy manifests as an outpouring of creative libido, strangely and powerfully attuned to the needs of the present moment. Idle daydreaming ceases, and the Mind turns full force to actively creating a willed future.

Distractions from one's Will become like painful shackles. Idle entertainment begins to be seen as a shameful waste of time and awareness. Being separated from this Ritual of Inevitability is like the separation of lovers. The Individual pines to return to their path, to their purpose.

In this zone, this magical circle of creation, the Individual embodies the Spirit of their immortal "I AM." As the focus of the Ritual moves in ever-tighter rotation around its objective, force begins building like the compounded tension accumulating in a bow. Like an arrow being steadily drawn and aimed, the power potential expressed in the Individual's gift is prepared for its delivery. Thus armed, the Individual can strike their target with the power of concentrated force.

With increasing practice, one's gift sets its aims ever higher, upward and beyond; in time to be shot forth with force as a masterpiece, a wonder, a work of genius—an effort of Earth aspiring to reach the Star of one's own excellence.

This Ritual is also the Hand, which is writing the book of one's existence.

In the shadow of these activities, the cosmic hand immortalizes the ritual's proceedings upon the universal aether. Each action is eternalized by its pen.

Thoughts become prayers directed towards the chosen attainment. Upon a small but passionately burning ember, the Individual's hopes are ignited. Like incense cast into the flame of one's being, billowing clouds of fragrant smoke come forth. There in that mysterious world of strange shapes, where imagination influences form, is the incarnation of one's idea. It is here, where one begins to make out the first hinting materialization of their willed vision. What was once just imagined is now beginning to take on a real shape. By virtue of the soul's willed aspiration the vision finally steps forth and begins to take on a life of its own.

True Will is this ember brought to life. Born of internal friction, its spark is conceived through the concentrated efforts of a repetitive ritual, where one's energy is applied as pressure upon a single point, rotating with the single-minded intention of igniting one's willed objective into existence. It is here that primitive memory recalls that intimate and ancient rite of survival—rubbing two sticks together to create the "need-fire."

Similarly, it is from a sort of psychological friction that this inner spark is created, a spark to life, ignited, carried on, and passed down from our ancestors.

It was while wandering through the dark and cold, and caught amongst unfavorable circumstances that our ancestors searched for the smallest fragment of dry material to perform this ancient rite. Likewise, we must also learn to use what we have to re-ignite this spark and survive, to carry on the flame.

It is with whatever is presently the most combustible part of Self that the Individual must use to perform this ancient ritual. A "ritual of need" connects us with deeply primitive and powerful unconscious forces of "adaptive Will" that lie within.

It is because of this spirit of "adaptive Will" that our ancient ancestors managed to survive and thrive amongst those early harsh conditions.

With this need-ritual mankind arose from being the prey of beast into a beast of prey. This is a purely human realm of creation. It is, perhaps, the most precious possession of humanity, and a defining characteristic of developing Mastery. Its spark ignites when the Individual learns to focus their energy to a precise, determined, and fertile point-of-action.

By focusing our energy in tight rotation around a given objective and applying pressure upon its chosen point, we eventually evoke the circumstances we have been seeking to create. Like the heat and fire produced by proper friction, persistence manages to ignite, in a moment of magic, those circumstances that the Ritual has sought.

We have inherited this capacity from our ancestors, a ritual evolved out of hunger, and desperation, and will-to-live and thrive. This kind of "adaptive will" is necessary to make dreams real—all out of sand, and mud, and ash, and ember, and soggy wet conditions, and obstacles, and ordeals that characterized the external conditions we meet in everyday life. It is from the Individual's Will that a blazing fire shall come forth, even out of wet tinder.

This fire must come forth, in time, through the Ritual. With cold hands and gnawing empty hunger—with nothing—the fire must be brought forth from one's own being. Like a child, it is conceived by the Individual's sheer lust for life.

The King of the Tribe is the One who can bring forth fire out of nothing.

A King brings forth the spark and carries the Fire. Without this Fire, one cannot be a King. From this magic was born the original reverence for all that is royal. It is this mighty act of applying knowledge, will, and skill, to bring forth the fire of creation that has rendered all that humanity has created with its own hands, and all that it has cherished.

It is those who, with Promethean spirit, pull down the fire of Heaven and claim it rebelliously as their very own spiritual possession who are the mythic Kings of Earth. It is these mighty Individuals who in turn use this fire to ignite their very own being, becoming as a fire themselves, a contagion of confidence in life.

Consumed by the desire to offer sacrifices to this self-created pyre, the Individual who sets the Will-fire alight does so with the divine fuel of self-belief. It is this belief whose substance gives life, and warmth, and hope to the tribe. The ability to do this is what marked the Magician-Kings of the past. The ability to perform this act is the establishment of civilization itself; it is the Ritual that marks the beginning of all that has been called Human.

The Sun rises again and again. The Ritual continues ever onward in the face of all obstacles, the boat of Ra passes through the infinite night.

Unendingly repeating: a beginning, a middle and an end. Destiny is an inevitability set in motion by the Ritual.

What might life bring?

This question elicits within consciousness an excitement, and also its primary fear—the fear of Life and its endless incarnations of events, from endings to beginnings.

This immense fear, both personal and universal, is a terror born of an unconscious lack of assurance, a failure of deep belief. It is, plainly speaking, the doubt of whether or not the Individual will be enough to overcome the situations they are destined to face in this life and beyond.

It is the fear of contending with the darkness that guards the gate to the Crown.

Held beyond this gate is the essential knowledge of truth. The guardian of this gate could be called many things as it takes the many forms of the Individual's most intimate fears.

The Crown makes itself known
when a voice from within roars:
"I WILL ALWAYS BE ENOUGH."

To affirm this belief, it is necessary to pass confidently through the shadow that guards this door of action and face the multifarious forms of fear acting as inhibitors of Self-Becoming. Up until that moment, the Individual secretly doubts themselves. With the death of this doubt goes the last remaining restraints upon potential development.

This Ritual is the primal act of Spirit leading to the Crown.

The "one who is King" is one who has discovered (and is comfortable demonstrating) that they will always be enough. Even in conditions that strip them naked and leave them cold and hungry, they can make fire.

If the need-fire principle is applied to the mastery of one's conditions, the Individual quickly begins to grasp the appropriate degree and nature of the force that need be evoked. It is through this practice that we become more efficient, and thus far more powerful in action.

The ritual requires discrimination and direction, only funneling one's energy into circumstances fertile enough to give forth the willed fruit. The Ritual is the vehicle of the Will, the medium for incarnating its aspiration. The Ritual represents the life of the Kingdom.

The Ritual is performed under the authority of the Crown. The Crown symbolizes that blooming awareness that one is, in themselves, enough to meet the demands of life. A King knows that when put in a position where they must do something, and where they must prevail... they WILL.

Having conquered this deep doubtful misconception of limitations, the Individual now may ascend to the circumstances ahead with a feeling of confidence, even in the face of conditions unknown. By a light-within, they are consoled!

Knowing the possible extent of their adaptivity to circumstances, they now can move boldly toward a mysterious new future. Presently uncreated, this future is to be hewn out of yet to arise events, the absolute composition of which there can be no true prediction of or real preparation for.

A King achieves this through the power of "the Ritual." That is to say—through the power of persistent and applied force. Through the repetition of intent, conveyed in all the available forms of action and languages of life, the Individual learns to express their WILL at every event.

CHALLENGE:

Application for Self-Initiation

Constructing a Ritual of Inevitability

Basic Concept: Your Evolving Ability Potential is the action of your deepest purpose, which is spawned by your immortal "I AM." Design your day with actions that match your intention. Cultivate the Seed-of-Self by committing to your gift.

Image: The hand that manifests "I AM." The spoke of the Wheel of the Great Ritual.

Objective: Commit to a daily ritual of skill development. Align actions with intent. Identify your gift, what psychologists call the Natural Lead Function by asking yourself "Where am I the most potent?"

Develop the latent powers within you, activate resources, and learn to use what you have. Establish a daily routine of developing resources and skills that will enable you to master the challenges required by your values. This is the ritual of manifestation.

Actions to take: Establish a daily routine of power by taking actions whose consistency will inevitably lead to the fulfillment of the "I AM" embodied in your symbol and story.

Crafting your Ritual is about designing your day. Put in place daily practices whose rippling effects will build into momentum. Set in motion a daily routine for generating this power. When seen as a Ritual that's giving life to your deepest purpose, a daily routine can sometimes lead to almost immediate rewards.

As you bring your symbol to life through daily actions, you gain the skills and resources required to fulfill your larger goals. Mastery involves the evolution of habit. Rituals are the active part of commitment. What are five commitments fundamental to the cultivation of your Seed-of-Self? What are the daily habits, rituals, or routines that will lead "inevitably" to your desired outcome? Consider your commitments, their accompanying actions and what these actions will lead you to become (richer, stronger, centered, more creative, etc.):

Commitments:

1._____

2._____

3._____

4._____

5._____

The Rituals:

1._____

2._____

3._____

4._____

5._____

A Bit of Science

There is a thing known as the "10,000-Hour Rule" that suggests after 10,000 hours of practicing some skill, a person's brain begins to function at a higher level, in time entering a terrain of mastery.

When we first begin something, we begin at what is called (in Neuro-Linguistic Programming) the level of unconscious incompetence, which means that we are making mistakes we don't even know we are making. But with applied effort, we become aware of our mistakes. This is called conscious incompetence. As we focus more on developing this skill, we begin to gain traction and improve—this level is called conscious competence.

After the skill has been honed, and we can perform its action well and with ease, we move to the level of unconscious competence, a point where our skill becomes second nature. This is the level of Masters. This is the model for any Ritual of Inevitably. Once we determine what we have set out to master we continue to rotate around that task like a bow wrapped around a stick creating a need-fire. It's the friction we apply through our efforts, coupled with the constant rotation of our lives around "the Ritual" that eventually ignites the spark whose first ember we nourish into the flames of Mastery. This is an ancient method of gaining power in the world—to select a worthy task and then, in the Roman style, beat it into submission. Mastery.

Something Mystical

A quote from Manly P. Hall in his lecture, "The Psychology of Religion Ritual."

"The validity of ritualism is sustained by a deep and abiding conviction that traditional ceremonies are important and significant and contribute to the security of the Individual's internal life. Rites and ceremonies can have a profound impact on psychological structures of those who perform them. Through the experience of daily rituals, the Individual can advance gradually from one state of consciousness to another. These rites and ceremonies and the myths that accompany them, tell the story of the growth and evolution of the consciousness of the individual who performs them."

My Experience

Ritual came early for me, when as a child, my grandmother first took me to Catholic Mass. Even though I found this ritual quite compelling, it wasn't until adolescence that I began to actively participate in rituals that I created myself. It was a deep and abiding fascination with Ancient Egypt that was responsible for my flowering interest in the occult, an interest that branched into nearly every relatable category.

Later, when I was twenty years old and living amongst a riotous mob in a dangerous urban environment, someone introduced me to the spiritual path of the Runes. The Runes encapsulate the wisdom of what might be called "the Viking way of life," a path that assumes hostility, risk, and adventure as part of the terrain of becoming your highest Self. The practical, survival-oriented perspective that the Runes offer was precisely the kind of spiritual path that my situation required. Unlike other paths, there are no assumptions that a "spiritual life" is necessarily a gentle life. In fact, the path of the Runes is one of bloody sacrifices. This early initiation into the wisdom of the Runes taught me that spirituality is not about just being nice and agreeable, nor is it about humbly making concessions to some god for the stain of sin. Instead it's about power. It is applied psychology, it's myth, sacrifice and ritual.

The Wisdom of the Runes teaches that real wisdom is gained from ordeals—powerful life experiences that never come without sacrifices. In the myths of the Vikings, many of the gods are maimed by their experiences, missing hands and even eyes. Their stories clearly demonstrate that we can never get something for nothing, the universe doesn't work that way. Real power must be earned, through initiation. Life is a Ritual of becoming, and that Ritual involves the sacrifice of many things: time, money, energy, and perhaps even parts of our Self.

Since those early days I have perpetually been involved in one initiation or another, one ritual or another, making mistakes and learning from them along the way. Today my life manifests the product of all those adventures in the form of a unique, self-created world view and spiritual path. At some point, life and "The Ritual" become one and the same, an eternal motion following the movement of the Sun.

SPIRITUAL KINGSHIP

Man is made for Gold

Onward forth!
the dawn of reclamation!
Claiming the full-inheritance,
of all that is SELF! By right-onward,
Anointed with this aspiration!
As a Conquer,
setting out to measure the territory,
tamer and master,
of their own consciousness,
proud and autonomous
bearing the CROWN
of Self-Created power,
of Individualized Force,
a Serpentine Halo,
like a Lamp!
The Sun of Self!
and its house of worship?
SPIRITUAL KINGSHIP
the alchemical way
whose process
multiplies the treasury
and purifies the Gold
of who
you are

THE CALL

INITIATION

CHAPTER SIX

The Crown of the Centralized Psyche

"A Kingdom divided in itself cannot stand."

–Thomas Hobbes, Leviathan

Passing through this gate implies "Authority granted." The will-to-become has slain all other thoughts.

At this new level of consciousness, the Initiate asks again, but this time more precisely, "What will be the central theme of life, around which everything else revolves? Where is that fixed point within consciousness, that immovable mountain that represents the authority within SELF?'

Previously the Individual had built a symbolic bridge by which the energy could cross from the powerful realm of the unconscious mind into conscious awareness. That energy could then be harnessed for use.

Now, the Pharaoh must unite these two lands, not only in spirit but also under one authority.

There can be no rebel causes allowed to run loose in the Sovereign Individual. No part of oneself may be allowed to play another part of oneself for a fool. To be divided against oneself is to be weakened, and ultimately defeated. A psyche divided against itself is torn from within, like a nation experiencing a Civil War. Whether it be a Kingdom's population or an Individual's psyche, that which is internally conflicted and incongruent *is at odds with itself.* In both cases, the cause is often found in the absence of a strong central authority. For the purposes of bringing order to our own consciousness, we will refer to this unification as The Centralization of the Psyche.

When wracked by internal disputes and a lack of coherent priorities the Sovereign State, like the Sovereign Individual, cannot stand. Such is the fate of both empires and Individuals who fail to centralize their mission and coordinate it with the true essence of their constitutions.

In metaphoric backdoor dealings, the incongruent person is self-hustled by conspiracies of their own design, foolishly committing betrayals of interest in exchange for contrite sympathies and meaningless votes. The gold that is "the good of the realm" is being bartered for "some silver to spend."

Debauchery of spirit quickly descends on the court in the King's absence: the dwarf mockingly wears the Crown. Busily the court moves to fruitless flirtations with sensation, the air fills with meaningless copper verbiage tossed to courtesans, "in exchange for a glance."

In the pursuit of leisure, the treasury has been emptied. The royal table is soiled with decadence, scattered with a mosaic disarray of over-consumption. Wax drips steadily from a candelabra, a rhythm quickened by a cold draft from an open window.

The first pungent stench from a candle, burnt to its end, can clearly be detected.

One by one flickering lights vanish from the hall as darkness begins to descend. It was such a lovely party.

Silk tablecloths sport the oil-stains of wasteful sacrifices. Flies buzz around the carcass of the feast. Numerous loaves of quick-staling bread grow stiffer by the moment, exposed to the air, and wastefully drenched in butter. Blurred vision begins to make out the forms of half-eaten remnants as the mind strains for clarity through cloudy memories of indigestible indulgences.

Like a rooster heralding the dawn, a hangover begins its loud crow. Here and there dim-staggering awareness begins to dawn, realities stumble forth. The musicians have stopped playing. Much wine has been spilled, and now, just now, being lost to audibility is the last sounds of those soft, tender, fleeing footsteps. The door is now being heard just as it shuts with their despondent exit, the women have all left.

This is the fate of both Empires and Individuals who let imprudence reign.

It's always in this lonely moment that the bill finally arrives, a financial statement that resembles a battlefield of mismanaged extravagance. Flanked while drunk, resources lie in ruin, mangled and broken. Casualties litter the periphery with little or no apparent reasoning behind their deployment. A quick glance at the cost on the receipt stirs strong emotions, coming on in waves, like the visceral image of unspeakable brutality, exaggerated numbers pile up like the bloodied corpses of loyal soldiers cut down in the fight-of-their-lives, with boots unlaced.

In this painful state, the divided individual realizes their efforts have been ineffectual, their aims abortive. What might have been a heroic fight now appears to be lost.

Such is the price of distracting amusements in the unruled Kingdom.

Priorities Must be Established. The Kingdom Must be Ruled.

Inner division and its threats must be squashed before the Kingdom can harness its reclaimed energy for expansion. It is unity of purpose that gives an Individual and their kingdom-of-being a true identity, and it is the Centralization of the Psyche that acts as a "Self-Suture." Before this centralization, one's consciousness is just a mass of swirling debris. Without sovereignty, there is chaos.

Suffering the disharmony of their disjointed complexity, and churning up chaos wherever they go, such a person simply conveys to the external world the lack of law that governs his internal world.

For the chaos of such a consciousness to become productive in creating itself in willed forms, one of its many parts, the strongest part, must step forward, amidst the swirling disorder, and claim the center. It is this part, like a mighty chieftain-priest, that establishes order. All those other parts become as servants whose lives revolve around the service of consciousness's primary objective.

This part that "claims the center" must be heartfelt for it represents the authentic essence of what you speak for. For a nation, this would be its capital. Its contemplation should stir strong emotions of passion and loyalty. This part becomes the center of a circle whose circumference includes the whole of consciousness. Establishing this sacred center, this Axis Mundi, is our core objective when we talk about the Centralization of the Psyche.

The organization of the psyche around a central understanding of itself is essential to establishing one's own "sacred order." As King of your own consciousness, it is from this place that you will rule. It is from this rooted vantage point that the King assesses the needs of the Kingdom, evaluating its parts, its immediate potentials, its long-term potentials, its immediate limits, its long-term limits, its available resources, and on and on. This is what gives consciousness "organization."

It is this organization, through the Centralizing of the Psyche that works to develop the Individual's gravity of purpose. It's this "gravity of purpose," and the mass that gravity attracts, that works as the axis around which all other parts of the psyche become orbital.

A King puts to iron and ash the disorder of conflicting interests. Discordant emotions and habits meet the guillotine. Setting out to weed the garden, a King tends the Kingdom with royal effectiveness, eliminating with righteous hand all breed of self-limiting beliefs that have been restricting their sovereign right.

The King is the Kingdom, the Kingdom is the King, both in body and spirit and experience. The spirit of the King represents that holy guidance for which nations once prayed.

To be a Sovereign Individual and a Spiritual King means the Individual must possess the ability to take command of present conditions, to apply concentrated force, to bring effective and adequate strength to the fight, and to endure until success is reached and complete. It is the embodiment of this spirit that makes a Man into a King. This task takes great strength, and that kind of strength requires an inner unity of purpose.

The ultimate purpose here is to develop one's "Spirit," so that whatever comes through the door, "I AM" is here to greet it, and at last, to prevail over it. That's a tall call, one that humiliates arrogance.

Arrogance is banished.
Confidence is asserted.

All the Individual can do?

IS ALL THAT THE INDIVIDUAL CAN DO!

It must really be the ALL.

Everything else does Fall.

The part of Self that stepped forward from chaos into the light of consciousness to bring order; that part who has survived all ordeals, who wins through its own efforts, who proves itself the strongest—that part alone can claim the right to be considered as a candidate for enthronement as the Individual's True Self.

The strongest part of oneself is the horse to bet on. No other part may stake a claim for the Crown. Attaining the Crown means that the Initiate has become a force of Nature—a Sovereign King amongst a consciousness firmly ruled. This allows a person to become the author of their own life, to write a book worth reading and to live a story worth remembering.

This path to the Crown leads up, up, up, at a very steep angle. Claiming your Crown means meeting it in its own home. We cannot just send a letter to God requesting our Crown. There's a special garbage can in heaven for passive prayers, which angels call "junk mail." Knowing that fortune favors the bold, we must storm heaven on our own initiative, go ourselves to that place so high, and (like Prometheus) defiantly claim it with our entire being.

The Primordial Hill

The Crown sits atop a summit called the Primordial Hill. To find it the Individual must discover their immovable center, which means they must hone down the central objective of their conscious existence. To understand oneself deeply, one must understand what rock their inner world revolves around for unity and order.

Symbolically, this mountain or Primordial Hill sits in the exact center of the Kingdom of consciousness. Its mass represents the "Original Self," the most ancient and primordial foundations of one's being. It's the place that has never moved, never been worn away. This place within consciousness can never be blown up, nor torn down, nor destroyed by elements or movements of Earth.

It's made of a material so primal and indestructible that of all that individual consciousness can know, of all the things that it can feel or think as a part of itself—this rock, this Primordial Hill, this mountain of primal Self is the only eternally established mass in the entire Kingdom.

All else will change. All else will be moved, someday. All else except this Primordial Hill which has stood ominously permanent from the beginning until the end, through cycle after cycle until the entire Universe has become what it once was not, has been turned inside out, has been drowned and burned and smashed to bits.

When the dust settles again, that mountain, that Primordial Hill upon which the Individual sets out to claim his rightful Crown, will stand and shall always exist. What exists there on that Primordial Hill represents what the Individual truly is, and yet is still unknown to them. They are formed of the essence of this unique yet unknown image. They cannot yet see it, but they can hear it—as a call to destiny.

The search for this place begins as the search for "the center" of consciousness. Relentlessly, one must seek this point within themselves, moving round and round in ever-tighter circles, continuously honing down on one's essential nature. The psyche, like a hunter's arrow, narrows the aim of its sharpened focus upon the target, bearing down on this central point.

Seeking this coordinate point in consciousness is a meditation; it encapsulates the Individual's thinking. The Mind revolves around this center. In this way, it resembles a mantra, a word that in Sanskrit means "a sacred utterance," a phrase intended to provide clarity and spiritual guidance.

The Identity Mantra: the one united goal of the Individual's being.

The Identity Mantra is formulated to answer the question: "What is my relationship to the Universe?"

This Mantra is an "Identity Mantra," a statement around which the Mind revolves to instill order and unity of purpose within. This Mantra is a vibrational furthering of the Individual's "I AM." Its composition, in both phrasing and tone, is structured as an affirmation of the one united goal of the Individual's being. However, this is more than a statement, it's a contract, a legal document verifying the Individual's law of authority on the inner planes.

Whereas the Flag of Sovereignty was the "the spirit of the law," the identity mantra is "the letter of the law." This law, of course, is not an external political law; it's on an entirely different plane. It's a "higher law," one that establishes order within the Individual's consciousness.

It is a pleasure to watch the chaos of one's inner world begin to take an ordered shape. As it does, clues as to the origin of its mysterious parts spring-up and make themselves known. Suddenly, things become apparent that were previously hidden. Unresourceful beliefs that unconsciously shaped the Individual's early experiences can now be seen for what they are. No longer just swirling blindly in the dark, the Individual finds that certain things can "have their place." Even what seems like a vice when uncontrolled can, in the right moment and properly applied, become something useful.

The Campaign: Mission Creates Meaningful Action

From this solid place, one now has a base from which to launch "The Campaign of True Will." Adventure waits on the horizon.

The Crown has been attained, and its centralized mission made sacred. Now it's time to make some important decisions.

The last phase revolved around the question, "What is the theme of Self and Life?"

The Primordial Hill has been mounted, its steep climb endured, and its Crown claimed. With this victory, the King has managed to establish a sacred order within consciousness. As he takes The Throne, the next question becomes, "Are all elements serving it?"

The Crown represents the attainment of intimate knowledge of our deepest purpose. It's to be enlightened to one's own consciousness aspiration. That is to say, The Crown symbolizes knowledge of one's primary function, their WILL.

This WILL is a statement to our ultimate priority in life. That priority is identical to the Individual's "will-to-become." Its attainment represents the highest value of individual existence.

This statement of Will, embodied in the Identity Mantra, is like the Individual's own Hammurabi. It is the authority of the Kingdom, the standard against which all are measured.

When consciousness is considering whether an action is "lawful" concerning this inner authority, the answer can be determined simply by asking whether it helps or hinders the central objective of consciousness. All thoughts not equated with its success are slain.

This central objective is the root verb implied in the Identity Mantra. To know this Mantra, which is like a chant of the Individual's spirit, is to be illuminated, and to repeat it is to forge a vibrational connection to the Immortal Self represented in the "I AM" statement.

As the Mantra spins the wheel within, it shucks off the weaker statements of internal dialogue as debris cast out into the asteroid belt of one's inner cosmos. As the Mantra is repeated its existence is affirmed and strengthened neurologically. Through constant repetition it begins to saturate consciousness, slowly seeping into the deeper regions of the subconscious mind where it will begin to effect a gradual change of inner being.

The Initiate who will be King must be capable of moving beyond doubt—the doubt about whether or not they possess this authority within themselves. To be able to operate without doubt, without hesitation, and without incongruence is the definition of Kingly action. It must emanate from a deep and pure place neither molested by common conventions nor castrated by common fears.

One must know beyond a doubt who they truly are, what they're truly capable of, and what they're most deeply driven to do. Equally, they must possess enough faith in themselves to do it.

Moving beyond doubt, this Individual boldly scales the mountain.

With the help of their Identity Mantra, they are nourished by a growing sense of inner enlightenment, along with a profound knowledge of who they are, a true understanding of their abilities, and a deep appreciation for the necessity of the vision that they are to produce. Willingly they have given themselves up to the great climb of life, affirming with their whole energy the pursuit of their attainment without fear or need to hold back anything in reserve.

This is the climb to the Crown; this is what it takes and what the path to Kingship truly calls for.

This is why it's the ultimate attainment, because the Man who passes these tests and overcomes these trials of spirit **becomes a King** through the ordeal of its initiations.

This Man is becoming a force to be reckoned with, virtually unstoppable in his chosen path, both one with the path and one with destiny... the creator and the created... the artist and the art.

Willumination

"The King is the Man who can."

-Thomas Carlyle

A King shines with Will-illumination. He *is* the source of authority, security, and power within his consciousness. Willumination is a symbolic transmutation. It represents the link between an Initiate's consciousness and the Solar Force. The Individual becomes a Sun—the central and ruling component of their own cosmos.

From a sure foundation, the King may now step forth, united by a knowledge rooted in the bedrock of Self and thus capable of rising to the highest peak of conscious aspiration.

The Crown: Self-Knowledge

The Crown is the attainment of the Centralized Psyche.

The Crown asserts the possession of self-knowledge beyond the surface of persona, a connection with the self-concept of one's primal being.

Attainment of The Crown allows the Sovereign to bring the future under his formative influence. Armed with this far-sighted perception, the affairs of life are tended as a bloom unfolding, synchronizing with the Individual's Will.

The Throne: The Evolving Ability Potential

The Throne symbolizes the mastery of something, a skill, a position, a way, a discipline. Whatever form it takes, it is an established position of power and the place from which to wield it. Some thrones are mightier than others. All thrones must, to some extent be defended. There will always be competitors because the Throne is a seat of power and a position of potential.

Thrones have always possessed deep connections with the idea of inheritance. Likewise, the skills which one builds their power upon in this world are most powerful when they are in close relation to the Individual's natural, inherited disposition. It is more effective to make good use of our own "natural terrain" than to strain endlessly to shape ourselves to that which we are not well fit. What skills match our natural disposition? To what kind of work are we best suited?

The Throne represents a skill developing into a grace. It is for mastery of a skill that we wish to be recognized. Happy is he who holds this cup, who understands himself deeply enough to choose the position of his Throne wisely!

It is in this stage that the natural lead function is honed, and acquired skills are crafted into a foundation for power. At a certain level, mastery of a skill involves the mastery of oneself, and hence one's Kingdom as a consequence. This is the link between the Kingdom and the Throne.

When choosing your Throne remember that it is *a practical seat of stable power*—and should be chosen for that purpose and situated in such a way that it can continue growing in might far into the future. Thus, it takes some deep thought and careful consideration. In order to find the proper fit it's necessary for the Individual to comprehend the nature of the work being chosen, including the sacrifices necessary.

The Kingdom: Actualized Experience

"It is a measure of the degree of strength of will to what extent one can do without meaning in things, to what extent one can endure to live in a meaningless world because one organizes a small portion of it oneself."

(Nietzsche, The Will to Power)

The Kingdom is the small portion of the world that one organizes oneself. In ancient Egypt, The Kingdom was also seen as the portion of the world brought to order by the King. Everything outside the borders of the Kingdom represented chaos.

The Kingdom represents the Individual's experience of life: their home, their affairs, their family and finance, and most importantly, their state of consciousness, the home of their existence.

When the King is good, the Kingdom is good. The King's body is the foundation of the Kingdom. The King's experience is the substance of the Kingdom. The King's vitality and well-being radiate outward magnifying the vitality and well-being of the Kingdom. As in ancient tradition, what is happening in the heart of the King is happening throughout the entire kingdom. The Kingdom is one's domain of consciousness. The enrichment of this Kingdom is the enrichment of the deep structure of the psyche itself.

The Crown helps us to unite our aims with who and what we (consciously and unconsciously) understand ourselves to be. Its actualization is the halo of self-realization. It addresses the question of what the individual thinks and feels about themselves. It represents the acceptance of all that one is being "Called" to do.

The process that will lead you to acquire your Crown, Throne, and Kingdom is outlined in this book. It begins with discovering the answers to the most important and practical questions of life.

1.) Who are you becoming in this life?

2.) What are you being called to do in this life?

3.) Where is the best place for living out this calling?

4.) How do you plan to master the requirements of this calling?

5.) Which resources are, or can be made, available to you?

...for the noble task at hand, which is:

To protect, maintain, and expand who you are, what you do, and where you can do it.

This mind-state represents both a perspective and a paradigm for understanding one's existence. It acts as a model for interpreting the meaning of particular events in life and defines a clear system of measurement for assigning those events a respective value. Spiritual Kingship codifies a philosophy, beckoning sovereignty, a spiritual path to which one willingly offers their oath of commitment once they begin to understand the priceless attainment that this unique way offers. Its noble disposition can then act as a frame of power through which to view everyday events—a corrective lens for bringing the unseen reality of Spiritual Kingship to life.

The model of Individual Sovereignty is a "Mastery Model." This Mastery Model is about enriching your representation of the World by enriching your internal representation of your Self. It works by recovering the missing pieces of psychological and spiritual wholeness and reincorporating this lost self-knowledge into the original sovereign state—the birthright of mankind. In effect, we are reclaiming the state of consciousness that existed before "the Fall."

As the story goes, when consciousness came to "know good and evil," a mythic separation occurred, a separation within the psyche. It resulted in a separation of conscious wholeness into good and evil, eschewing their interrelation and interdependence.

The price of this tasting of forbidden fruit was the acceptance of sin, a three-letter word that condemns almost all original impulses. As Sovereignty was mankind's original state, it was the idea of sin that led man to question his rightful sovereignty. Unsure of his worthiness and shackled by doubt, man attempts to reclaim the garden degenerated from Cain down through all of man's descendants. Then as is today, once you have a person questioning whether or not they possess natural sovereign rights they are within arm's reach of slavery.

In this way, Mankind first fell from an original sovereign state into a place of litigation, a place where the legitimacy of his power was to be questioned, a hobbled position requiring him to formulate justifications and reasons in defense of his claims, a court battle of internal monologue that would ever after struggle to retain even partial ownership of that original, rightful inheritance.

This shadowy iron gate of self-doubt about the legitimacy of one's own Will, that doubtful questioning of whether one's inherent nature is "good" or "evil" is the same doubt still being leveraged today to bring the Individual under external control.

Doubt Divides the Crown

Doubt divides the Crown and melts it down into trinkets for the masses. It takes the Individual's Sovereign right and distributes it. Doubt divides the crown, but with the best of "democratically minded intentions" of course!

In truth, it is but paying homage, to the abased and incoherent vices of the peasantry, to a meager and valueless reality which represents the weakened impulses of a divided self. It's this divided self, which like the Phantom Self, must be rounded up by the King, and hanged.

The Crown symbolizes sovereignty, which represents the symbolic "highest value" to a King. For the Sovereign Individual, it also represents the oath taken to themselves; it's a devotion to their own becoming.

To trade the gold of self-rule for social approval is to squander what is eternal and complete for what is transitory and partial.

To "democratically" hand over responsibility for one's life is to cast pearls before swine, and power before emptiness. To feel the need to take consensus before every action, to be censored by a conformity to mass appeal, to negotiate with the negligible complaints of the constantly complaining, to remain recalcitrant to the authority of one's own heart, in short, to dismiss the divine right to assert the Will of one's own sovereign consciousness, is to surrender the deed to one's soul over to commercial developers and to aggrandize the ignorance that threatens to strangle the world.

To hand a thing of such immense value over to the World is to debase it. Never could the herd conceive of the true value, true purpose, or true potential of a thing such as Sovereignty unless they someday make that journey of conquest themselves and come to know it by what it costs. Sovereignty is Gold.

Historically, attempts to reveal the inherent gold of self-sovereignty and the priceless value of the immortal "I AM" (to the masses) have been met by crucifixions, outrage, and mob violence. For the Sovereign Individual to claim that such an attainment is possible and yet still outside the reach of the ordinary bloke, is to rebuke the eternal wails of blame and resentment that are the trademark of the masses. History's pages are dog-eared with the martyred corpses of those rare, fine specimens who have shone brightly enough to have stirred outrage among the common folk. The Sovereign Individual, on the other hand, understands the personal responsibility each man holds for their own growth.

Because this responsibility appears so less desirable than the power that it yields, the many-faced herd tends to see sovereignty only as riches to be plundered, and with mob mentality only seeks to pull this Crown down from its heights and cash in on its divinity as if it were just scrap metal. They will see its value only for the wine and women they can attain with it.

Like every religion that has emerged since the veiling of the ancient mystery schools, the attempts to serve the true spiritual need of humanity have had to contend with the lower orders of base ambitions.

Pity and charity mock the nobility of the recipient's spirit. Handouts to base impulses only serve to keep the dejected parts of one's character hanging on. The Sovereign Individual chooses only to serve the highest part of themselves.

The Sovereign must avoid feeling pity, even for the weaker parts of their own character. These longtime habits are like shady but outwardly sympathetic friends—nodding while we rant, pretending to care while we complain, and all-the-time committing petty thefts calculated to occur so that we do not notice—until it's too late. Such an ignoble part of one's character has no place in the King's court.

It's in wanting to make the crooked appear straight that a sympathetic heart deceives itself.

Etymologically, even our words for truth and honesty demonstrate this. To be "true" means that one could distinguish a straight board from one with a curl, and could construct a building that was straight, level, and square. From this we also get the phrase "to look one square in the eye."

Thus, to be an "honest" man implies the quality of keen judgment, that symmetry of understanding required to "hone" a true block. In this regard, the construction of the Ancients remains unsurpassed.

In the time of the pyramids, what man created was "true," because he understood the laws of nature. Only truth endures, hence, what ancient man created was well built. To achieve this sort of eternality of structure, what man builds must be founded on an accurate understanding of the world, a true perspective. Otherwise evidence of man's eschewed judgment will be built into everything he creates. As it is today.

Before truth became a subjective preference, it was a mathematical and architectural fact. Let us once again begin to construct monuments (and truth) that can endure.

Sovereignty is that which distinguishes itself from the shoddy workmanship of the "vulgar." It's the better part of oneself.

Of all the mythological forces that have been set against it, it was those commonplace, dirty-faced, base desires that originally broke the Crown. The stubby hands of ignorance took the Crown from its place, dropped it, and it was halved; then stolen and melted down by thin-greedy fingers.

The Gold that was the original Crown was broken down into ever-smaller factions and into fractions; smaller and smaller currency, being mixed with the intentions of inferior metals.

In time, the purity of its lofty value was lost, and instead of the proud command of Sovereignty that shines like the Sun, the copper penny of consensus became the common currency.

Circulated wealth is now in penny-stocks.

The original Sovereignty of the Sphinx has been defaced, and desert-worn. The King's tomb has been robbed. The eternal pyramids are now missing their limestone casing and golden capstones. The royal treasures have been exhumed, confiscated, and their meaning re-interpreted to serve the debauched needs of contemporary dispositions.

A desperate need to validate these crimes has mostly rallied around sacred forgeries, hastily gathered documents compiled by interest groups, religions rubber-stamped with counterfeit miracles, deeds to power photocopied on cheap paper bathed in Wite-Out. The spiritual might of sovereign right has been subsumed by way of an out-of-state transfer of sacred authority into the hands of a stranger known only by an alias.

It is this ravenous cannibalism of sovereign power that must forever justify its illegitimate existence by claiming to have been a victim of this same power, and thus reasoning itself to be entitled to its appropriation. Despite the historic catastrophes perpetrated by the mutiny of guerrilla groups who claim ascendance in the vacuum of legitimate authority, the consolidated power of the Sovereign has yet to reassert its rightful claim to the Crown. Mythologically speaking, the battle between Horus and Seth is imminent.

As these politicized bands of murders and thieves divide the spoils of their precious plunder their soiled consciences still necessitate they mutter halfhearted reconciliations to themselves and others, "the Eternal Pharaoh," they say with bloody hands, "*had* to be dethroned for the good of all."

It is now, in the absence of a rightful King, that the merchant emerges: foreign to the land, suspiciously wealthy, and conspicuously interested in helping, now wishing to offer the recently robbed a good deal. The merchant smiles, repeatedly addressing with the phrase, "my Friend."

The solid gold of Sovereignty has found its replacement, in Hollywood. Celebrity now presents itself as Sovereign of the World, a shiny but deceptively thin-plating over a weak and corrosive core of cheap substance.

"So many base plated coins passing in the market, the belief has now become common that no gold any longer exists—and even that we can do very well without gold!"

-Thomas Carlyle, On Heroes

The outer shine of persona is a thin plating: the throne of marketing, the crown of the merchant, an act put-on to cover bankruptcy with the thin skin of a flattering exterior.

Persona seeks to inflate perceived value while carefully hiding itself with distractions of the eye. A clever persona is as trustworthy as a gypsy pickpocket.

The King's charisma, however, represents solid securities: a divine gift, a majestic reflecting of inner light, a warm glowing sun that shines its redemptive light upon the kingdom.

The marketing of majesty is less about the "Crown of Enduring Value" and more about the clink of profits rumbling into the hands of merchants whose golden exchange is that of a mere headdress, a power procured through the rhinestone cunning of quick sales.

The Conclusion? Suspect all that outwardly glitters, of fraud, until proven pure by test absolute.

This fronting of worth, this sandbagging of substance rules the marketplace. The call of every commercial carries its tone. It's surface appeal, a transitory vanity, a set of dazzling reflective mirrors casting images in a grotesque distortion of the truth. It manages, however, to make itself profoundly appealing with catchy jingles and cheap smiles.

Merchant-kings have become the premier post-modern magicians, living by the art of smoke-and-mirrors, buttering their bread through clever orchestrations, marketing their social power through seductively seditious, though entertaining acts. With a wealth of stage make-up, they perform.

Fantasy exists to be captivating; thanks to Hollywood the lives of fictitious characters captivate our emotions. The show must go on, lest the audience awaken from its trance. At all costs, this new reality must be entertaining, must be able to support a suspension of disbelief strong enough to prevent the enamored from seeing through the ringmaster's outward mask, and into their conniving heart. Feast your eyes on a photoshopped reality in high-definition.

With a silver-tongued cunning the deception of the persona envelops itself around potential authenticity like a strangling vine. But in truth, the ability to cultivate a surface appearance without revealing the fragility and hastiness of its construction has become essential to the business of life.

No one is saying to stop fooling the World, it's merely being suggested that one double and triple check to make sure that one is not fooling oneself! Neither should one be content to be fooled by the World, or its deceiving merchants who play King.

Persona and high-finance live by the same meat, they are the arts of cultivated inflation, craftsmen at deceiving perception, carefully cloaking important details that could reveal their inventory of assets to, in truth, be but cleverly packaged liabilities.

Divided, the partisan forces bicker. At every opportunity they seek to infect the Sovereign Individual, trying to dissolve their consolidated power into a fragmented multitude of external forms whose manipulation rewrites the ledgers of Sovereign accounting to formulate imaginary debts. These imagined debts and their mounting interest can then be used as evidence that the Individual's dealings are better to be relinquished to outside communal control.

The beast these types fear most is the Sovereign Man, that spiritualized Individual who is an Authority unto themselves and so cannot be externally controlled by the usual manipulations.

The spirit of the Sovereign is in itself a force of Nature, a representation of the eternality and goodness of a thing that cannot be persuaded from the context of its being.

Likewise, this is the life and eternal power of elemental fire, water, earth, and air. No amount of propaganda or bribery can work against the nature of a thing elemental in itself.

It is self-doubt that opposes the original sovereign state. It's the seeds of this doubt, cast broadly by the architects of chaos, that gave rise to the diabolical landscaping of thorny hedges called "uncertainty."

For millennia it was the King who was the source of certainty. The King represented the archetypal man, and in playing this role he was also man's connection to the cosmos.

But when the ancient rite was no longer performed, when the teachings were no longer passed on, when the King no longer ruled, when there was no one remaining who was qualified to carry the torch of civilization, the light began to die. With neither light nor hero to resurrect the faith, actors stepped in to play the part temporarily. There was no longer an incarnated King to reestablish the certainty that is the fruit of wisdom and the cornerstone of civilization.

In the absence of an incarnated King to bring order out of chaos was born the post-modern era, and our noble task—to make ourselves in the image of that standard, to bring order to the Kingdom of our consciousness.

To resurrect this Sovereign spirit the Individual must strike out into the great expanse of their potential and conquer it. On this road, they are strengthening themselves for the test that will again lead to the Crown. Onward the Sovereign Individual moves, both inwardly and outwardly conquering all that presents itself as a noble challenge.

The Campaign of True Will is the active assertion of the spirit expressed in the Flag of Sovereignty and its symbol.

To become the conquering light, one must also incorporate and learn to use the powers of darkness.

Both light and darkness are part of life. Equally, they are a part of one's being.

Mastering one's own darkness means a confrontation with the shadow side of self. This confrontation, which must occur, is also a confrontation with the realities of pain set against the Individual during the process. It involves facing a chilling fact: there exists a frightening darkness that can be neither avoided, nor repressed, nor can it ever be fully extinguished. It can only be incorporated. To fear it, or to be infected by its doubt, is the contagion that first quarantined the Individual from their original sovereign state, and from "the Garden."

Like Chiron the kingly centaur with his un-healing wound, life will always find a way to bring the consciousness of pain into our awareness. A stiff refusal to acknowledge this fact will only bring fear and retreat when it shows itself. The acceptance of this fact means that the Individual who "takes their lashes," undeterred and unrepentant, can continue on to the glory of their own self-made heaven. It is this Solar Man who has become a representation of his own God, the light of his own Sun. Past the fear he moves, conquering all in the name of all that he knows himself to be, seizing all opportunities that make themselves available.

This breed of Individual is making themselves unstoppable. They will no longer be fenced by pain or the threats of pain; no longer be baited with pleasure or promises of pleasure. Such a person is making themselves inwardly self-contented and powerful.

From the fortress of this self-contentment their Will may strike like lightning from the heights of their psycho-spiritual independence; and down into the World, whose passivity and doubt look forever skyward for something strong, certain, and forceful to worship, and to save them.

CHALLENGE:

Application for Self-Initiation

Centralizing your Psyche and Claiming your Crown

Basic Concept: Spiritualize your Mission. Hone down the central objective of your existence—identify what all else rotates around for unity and order. Sovereignty is the life-giving Sun of internal stability and order, the primordial foundation of Self.

Image: The Primordial Mountain within, the Crowned peak.

Challenge: Centralization of the psyche represents the attainment of your "Crown." To claim your "Crown," you must capture the mantra of your being in a phrase that unifies the Mind and connects it with your True Identity and Mission.

Like the Tibetan monks in their caves chanting "Om Mani Padme Hum," imagine this phrase as vibrating from your secret center and radiating outward.

Action to take: To do this, hone down your inner truth into an "Identity Mantra" that is a statement about, and an oath to, your SELF.

To unveil your mantra ask yourself, "What is the most solid statement I can make about my innermost nature and objective? Who do I think I am? What do I believe I'm here for? What's the one-line bio for my True Will, aka the life I want to lead?"

My Identity Mantra:_____

This mantra acts as a reminder of the "oath" you are keeping with your-self. Keeping your mantra central in your mind keeps your deepest knowledge of who you are, and your Mission, close at heart. Your Identity Mantra is a stable center around which the mind can orbit during chaotic moments. Make it a habit of repeating this phrase often. As you do, refine it to deliver the most potent effect.

Extracting the gold of who you are, by embodying it in a mantra, helps you connect and identify with your Mission. The "Crown" is a symbol of your masterful achievement; you are now becoming fully identified with your True Will. The epic story of your life is unfolding. Claim your Crown.

A Bit of Science

Schizophrenia is defined as a sense of mental fragmentation, a mentality characterized by inconsistent or contradictory elements. The word liter-ally means "split mind." Centralization of the psyche is the opposite of schizophrenia. Centralization of the Psyche means putting all of one's psychological components in accord with a central ideological prin-ciple—that of their own life's purpose as embodied by their True Will.

Whereas schizophrenia is characterized by inconsistent or contra-dictory elements, Centralization of the Psyche is the culmination of a ritual whose intention is to Will One Thing, to make all one's thoughts, words and deeds consistent with that Will and to reconcile the contra-dictory elements in a person's psyche so that all the duality inherent in life and reflected in human nature can be transformed from contradic-tory to complementary. It's like the coming together of both the left and right hand to participate in cooperative action. That action is the ritual, and its aim is the "Centralization of the Psyche."

Something Mystical

Long before there was psychology there was religion. Before religion there was spirituality. They have all claimed an intention to help mankind with their struggles. The problem for humanity has remained much the same through these transiting methods.

Freudian Psychology looks at man as a specimen, full of pathologies to be worked on over countless hours of psychotherapy. Religion, for the most part in the West, looks upon man as something of a parasite, crawling in acquiesced submission to an omnipotent God that it constantly fails to please. Older than the other two: spirituality is the primeval root, which has taken many forms. Today its molested essence is embodied in the three "faiths" that currently dominate (sometimes subconsciously) almost all areas of culture and politics.

What we are to touch upon here, however, is a spiritual path that stems from that same primordial root and yet sits astutely between the other two. While many who search for literal interpretations miss the mark, the truth for which we seek is available only to those capable of reading between the lines.

In an ancient manuscript called "The Sacred Magic of Abramelin the Mage" is the description of a ritual (by a man named Abramelin) acquired somewhere in Egypt during a long spiritual pilgrimage from Europe. What he proposes is that each Individual has what could be called a "Holy Guardian Angel": a concept with many of the same attributes of the Greek daemon, the unified self of Jungian psychology, the higher-self of new-age thought, as well running parallel to the idea of a personal muse or genius.

Although Abramelin's ritual is highly involved and time-consuming, requiring the Individual to spend six months in near-total solitude performing ritual preparations and attaining profound meditative states to at last attain communion with the Holy Guardian Angel, its success and effects have been acknowledged by some very noteworthy Individuals.

Whatever one wishes to call that particular force of consciousness, its effect is to raise the Individual to the level of a Sovereign, a divine instrument, and to align the Individual's every thought, word, and deed with its higher calling, its Will. This, of course, can have a very powerful and profound effect on that individual and what they are capable of.

In a world where constant distraction has become a "disorder" and chronically searching the internet for life's answers has become a syndrome of mass spiritual abdication, this type of spiritual awakening is all the rarer. By comparison to the masses who are ever at the feeding trough of social consensus and divergent agendas of media manipulation, the Individual who "knows themselves," and learns to connect with an inner source of authority and guidance, can realize their life task and become a near godlike being in their psycho-spiritual essence.

In short, to be able to think for yourself outside the box, to be motivated by a deep sense of purpose that you have personally discovered, and to be able to focus your life around the attainment of a true and noble objective is, in this day and age, more than just an indication of genius, it's as close to divine as anything else that currently exists.

My Experience

I have admittedly had the luxury of spending the last twenty-five years absorbed in these studies, but it has been a luxury that has come at a high cost. I forfeited many things: money, relationships, friends, stability, ease, comfort, popularity, community, all because I chose to follow the breadcrumbs of this journey over all else.

Likewise I have spent years wandering, living in radically experimental intentional communities, risking all, throwing caution to the wind, following subtle impulses, wandering without place or home, experimenting with various "states," reading massive volumes which no one in my company cared for or wanted to hear about, entertaining taboo concepts, following little known spiritual practices, creating artistic works, performing strange and involved rituals, and generally walking the edge of ideas that many people fear and shun.

There were moments, to be sure, a plethora of moments indeed when my decision to follow this path seemed to have been wrong. There have been trials, both figurative and legal in which it seemed that I should not have followed my True Will.

But, I did it anyway, and I kept doing it despite the protests of "sensible" people, and the doubts arising from my own encounters with darkness, and the prolonged rebuttals from those who wished to frame my disposition in a way that made their own complacency more tolerable.

The result? I came to understand that I am being moved by a powerful force, one that can not be deterred or suppressed. Along with this came the knowledge that neither the promise of pleasure nor the threat of pain has the power to dissuade the Sovereign Individual from their path. In truth, nothing can be offered that is as valuable as maintaining contact with the source of life within, nor can the world ever provide real estate as valuable as the mythic world composed of one's own conscious being.

INITIATION

CHAPTER SEVEN

Attain a Meta-Vision

"You shall, I question not, find a way to the top if you diligently seek for it; for nature hath placed nothing so high that it is out of the reach of industry and valor."

-Alexander the Great

A King is an Individual who possesses a powerful experiential contact with the Sun within, a center inhabited by a force completely unmovable, eternal, and unique. Through word and deed, a King transmits that force into the World. In this grand respect, there is the recognition that the King's Will is the earthly echoing of the great Will of the Universe.

As an agent of destiny, one's acts become sacred. To others, this anointed Individual is seemingly self-serving, yet they understand themselves to be a servant of the cosmos. From the viewpoint of others, this "service" is simply self-pleasing rhetoric, yet within the Individual's consciousness, they live as a self-willed prophet whose True Will represents the worship of an unseen order of the cosmos.

The King's Energy is the link between the Individual's Will and the necessity of the Universe.

The Sovereign Individual is able to experience an awe-inspiring connection between their own Individual Will and the necessity of the Universe—both being fulfilled by the same act.

A Sovereign Individual is no longer just another human parasite crawling about the earth seeking to complete disjointed fantasies. Nor is he a puppet content to parrot politically correct commandments, nor a mouthpiece for the interest and arguments of the lowest common denominators. Instead, the Individual has become a vehicle of Will, a manifestation of the incarnated Sun.

This is the beginning of an Earth-shattering experience, as well as the dawning awareness of a new perspective: that of The Meta-Vision.

The Meta-Vision

The Meta-Vision represents the expansive sight gained from the summit of the Primordial Mountain. It is a Vision granted from up above, the privilege of those who make its epic climb. Its gaze burns as the Initiate's third eye, granting a glimpse of a reality existing "between the lines."

In this formative dimension, collected possibilities and elemental potentials meet. The Initiate's awareness opens up panoramically from what was previously the cramped constriction of a mere window view. Suddenly a new reality emerges. With eyes stretched open wide, the Initiate experiences an expansive realization of the existence of previously hidden potentials forming on the horizon.

A demiurgic flood of consciousness overwhelms imagined limitations with the force of previously unperceived possibilities. Such an experience has the power to shock and to awaken the Individual to the dawn of a new day. With a bursting forth of light and sound the Meta-Vision grants the Individual a glimpse of what is destined to come, a trumpet eternally announcing how much more lies ahead.

Even with the great length of the journey traveled so far, by comparison, the experience of the Meta-Vision reduces both the size and importance of one's previous journey to seem as not more than a drop in the bucket of what's to come. All events so far have been just a preparation for this dawn.

It becomes clear that this new dawn is more than just another page in the story of one's life. It's a whole new chapter in an epic myth, a continuing saga of one's struggle toward an inevitable victory whose screenplay is the Individual's Grand Vision. This is the true beginning of real beginnings. All else has been just a rehearsal for this production.

Once received, the Meta-Vision must also be digested and its nourishment extracted. Fed by this vision, the Sovereign takes their rightful place amongst the Kingdom and begins their reign in true.

Symbolically, the wheels of the King's chariot, like the wheels of the Individual's own strategic actions, must begin moving forward in the direction of some landmark on the horizon. Like the chariot, the Campaign is a vehicle to power. The movement of this chariot represents timely action, seizing opportunities as they are forming.

Reality is marked by change; mastery means developing an opportunistic approach to this change.

The campaign's chariot must keep moving, just as the Individual must continually free themselves from the gravity of inward sluggishness—that rutted depression into which the wheels of so many ventures become sunk in the lethargy of lost momentum. Things must keep going lest they succumb to the weight of gravity, and the inertia of their own stubbornness.

It is that stagnating force of inertia that forsakes the faint of heart in the swamp of their own sorrows—sorrows born of castrated hopes and abortive efforts. Here, in this muddy battlefield, many have gotten hopelessly stuck.

To begin something, especially something as great as conquering oneself and one's conditions, takes immense energy. More energy than most mortals believe they possess. For many, the quest seems IMPOSSIBLE. For the weak of heart, it will not happen. Yet, succeeding in this quest means that a transformation has truly taken place, and there is no longer anything "common" about such a transformed Individual.

It is through the archetypal process of initiation that the Individual is transformed into the body and blood of the King—and in this process transforms their life into a sacrament in the form of a universal solar experience. The energy of the sacred King awakens and becomes activated in the heart and mind of the Individual. This is the religion of Kings, a holy path that had previously lived dormant in the blood of the Initiate.

Now, charged with this force, life becomes a game of completion— a test to live in accord with an inner harmony. Inspired by a Grand Vision, the Will of the Sovereign is empowered with the capacity to apply its force. Its process is at once the meaning, the goal, and the gift of consciousness.

Through each phase of life, and at every challenge, transactions of the soul occur. They are written upon the universal aether of the Individual's unconscious mind. It is the ledger of the sacrifices and exchanges made at every leg of the journey. The efforts recorded in this ledger and the entries and deposits made "under the account of True Will" are the only actions that the Individual can consider as investments—because they are the only type of deposit whose worth gains in accumulated interest.

However, if some person had really found themselves to be just a commonplace mortal, just a person, just a persona, just a personality and nothing more, then they would be among the litter of broken bones, shattered relics, and abandoned dreams that lie discarded along the roadside of this intimately challenging path. Such a "person" would not be centralized and would not be the solar star of their own unique system. Their internal structure would not be organized around their True Will, and their design would not reflect the motion of a universe. Their inner world would not be the source of its own light. They would not be harmonized by a holistic purpose. They would not be a creative force of life.

They would be nothing more than debris cast aside. They would lie scattered in the sands, smashed to bits by their own internal conflicts. They would be discarded as abandoned dreams whose failure is that the dreamer did nothing more. They would be shattered relics of a thing which could not evolve, could not take to a new shape, and could not apply itself in a new way to the evolving conditions of a journey that demands of its traveler a constant gymnastic flexibility of spirit and ability.

If instead of ascending and opening one's eyes to a Grand Vision, if instead of taking up authorship and authority of one's own life, if instead of properly managing one's conditions, if instead of being a true Individual and becoming the living image of an Immortal King— if instead of this a person chooses the path of submission to consensus and forfeits their potential for society's guilt-ridden liabilities, then their Crown shall be nothing more than scrap metal awaiting the blast furnace.

This effectively neutered "citizen of the world" is neither a King, nor a Sovereign Individual, nor a self-creating spirit. In short, their existence is of no consequence in the King's Game. They are a pawn on their own chessboard. Could this pawn really be the True Self? No amount of pawns, however loud their cries, can ever equal the voice and authority of a King. How many people today claim to be unique individuals who are but a parade of pawns wearing tinfoil crowns? How many lost souls does it take to wrestle the reins of personal choice from the hands of a Sovereign Individual?

Under such conditions, how long could a Kingdom stand and endure? How long before the wheels of the King's chariot sink into the quagmire of "group think?" How long can the King entertain a horde of bickering commentary before the morale of his army sinks? Unless the Individual remains committed to their Grand Vision and forward momentum is constantly being generated throughout life, the Kingdom will succumb to this atrophy.

It's in spite of this outward pressure to yield, that the Sovereign Individual commits themselves to the fulfillment of the purpose for which they have been designed and created—that of maintaining forward momentum in the Great Campaign.

Even with a Crown, life does not just simply comply without the wily forces of wit, will, and charm. The challenges have, in fact, only just begun. This is sure to be dawning on the Individual who now has the advantage of a new and farsighted perspective.

Although no longer blinded by immediate circumstances, the Individual who manages to attain an overview of the larger conditions involved is now courted by the cognition of things previously unknown.

There may be many potentials in formation whose future demands (by comparison) dwarf the most immediate and apparent "needs" currently realized.

Likewise, the transitory fantasies seeming so important and appealing during early phases can now be seen from a truer perspective. All of those little pleasures and habits sacrificed for Kingship, whose separation was first felt like such a loss, are now as if found in an attic box with a binky and a baby blanket—embarrassing attachments to what previously were but infantile pacifications. In the Individual's spiritual adolescence these crude enjoyments were held as gold, whereas now they can be seen for the gaudy jewelry that they are.

With growing consciousness of future possibilities, the Individual gains an advanced awareness of unformed needs. They begin to intuit things presently hidden from the sight of the uninitiated and learn to adjust themselves to the possible outcomes that may arise from these new developments. It's this advanced cognition that the King uses to see the Campaign through its inevitable battles and through to victory.

This victory of aspiration synthesizes the Grand Vision with the mood of the New Constructive Myth. The myth is living, unfinished is its "book of revelations." The Individual's story is building onto another and another one of its multiple climaxes.

Rising again and again from the deflation of giving ALL, the King finds the Will and its lust-to-become returning stronger each time. Resolute is the King's stature and pose. The King maintains this state, in the worship of vital strength. He welcomes the challenges of life with an increased circulation of blood, and breath. All to penetrate ever deeper into the mystery of Will. It is through the joy of the WILL's ever-increasing satisfaction that the Individual is inspired to attain their life's ultimate purpose.

This Individual who seeks inspiration comes to find it in each breath. With every rise and fall of the chest, progress is made. This inspiration becomes the force that perpetuates the Individual's life, the divine wind that fills the sails of their uniquely inspired True Will.

In the very breath we breathe lives the source of inspiration as we may want or need!

This inspiration is "unto another final chapter of resolution," and even unto another final page, whose last word represents the complete expression of the Grand Vision.

All of life up until now can be reduced to a headline, a one-liner, or at most the first page of a book.

Opening again and again as the great book of existence —it is the self-willed story being written on internal pages of the Individual's intimate world.

Step-by-step and phase-by-phase the Sovereign Individual fulfills their destiny by committing to writing this saga of the Immortal Self unto its completion.

Taking up the authorship of life, and composing each incantation of the Will poetically, one becomes an artistic authority. This means using the guile of art, composing one's words as magical incantations designed to arouse the Eros of nature herself. In this way, her will is aroused to copulate with the King's, and both nature and psyche are moved to respond equally.

Thus, in harmony with nature, the Individual magnifies their Will, which is also a calling forth of the will of Nature herself. The path of True Will might even be considered an exaltation of the will of Nature. She is the Great Mother and the one who originally gave birth to the primacy of the Individual's natural Self.

It is Nature herself, the wisdom and knowledge of Isis, whose love grants the Individual a glimpse into that veiled purity which is the womb of the Individual's natural being.

The King completes the book of existence; even unto the last word, even unto the very last letter of the final sentence, even unto the last period, which marks the end and an initiation into a new and seductive beginning.

Who but the Sovereign Individual has the WILL and the courage to stand in the face of all they fear and commit to the task of affirming their divine right, of completing their Saga?

It has only been weakness, and misguided sympathies, and sentimental weight, like accumulating trash that had defiled the Temple.

WHO SHALL PROCEED INTO THE MOUTH OF
THE BEAST,
WITHOUT ANY EXTERNAL REASSURANCE
THAT VICTORY IS EVEN POSSIBLE?
WHO HAS CONQUERED THE FEAR OF THE ABYSS?
-THAT UNSPEAKABLE TERROR
THAT LIES BETWEEN MANHOOD AND
GODHOOD

The only thing that prevents the nightmarish disturbance of future disasters from becoming widespread panic and societal breakdown is the vagueness of conviction which affects ninety-nine out of a hundred individuals in the postmodern era.

It is the one percent Individual who transcends the common mass in depth of being and breadth of vision—it is the rare Individual who will claim their Crown.

The Sovereign Individual "knows something" that others apparently do not. They "understand something" that others are apparently ignoring. This grants the Sovereign a power, which apparently escapes others. It's the power of having a "Grand Vision."

Define your Kingdom

The Primordial Hill represents a centralized state of consciousness, one's very own Mt. Sinai. It must become anchored in the Individual's awareness. It's from this centralized point within that the messages from the unknown Self are received, that a new level of awareness is announced.

The Royal Perspective

Like a circling hawk from up above, who sees both the broad expanse of the horizon and the acute detail of the landscape below, the Initiate must develop the ability to set goals within the wholeness of an overall mission. It's within the context of this mission that strategies are formed, formulated to manifest the symbolic completion of one's Grand Vision. From this heightened perspective, the boundaries of the Kingdom can be accessed, and the territory of one's future rule familiarized.

Upon the Primordial Mountain, the Sovereign
is Granted a Glimpse of the Horizon that
Represents their True Potential.

Keeping one eye always on the bigger picture and the other eye focused on the emerging matters at hand, it becomes possible to synthesize a perspective which includes both the immediate and the far-off to better manage affairs. This is the "royal perspective," and its strategic function is symbolized by the astute vulture.

It is the vulture, who sits perched in silent observation of all-terrain, wasting not one ounce of energy on fruitless chases but waiting for the ripe fruit to fall on its own before plucking the bones. The vulture was a royal symbol of ancient Egypt, worn alongside the uraeus serpent on the headdress of the Pharaoh. Equally, it was an emblem closely associated with the energy of the Queen.

This is the power of the quiet opportunist, of the royal kind. It's the vulture who waits patiently for the right moment, who swoops down when the work shall be swift, when the prey has not even the strength to stand, when resistance has waned to its lowest point, when the fight is already won, when the ready harvest seems near effortless to gather that it enjoys its feast.

In his famous book, *The Art of War*, author Sun Tzu called this "the art of winning without winning." It's the art of strategic maneuver, the art of opportunism. The ancient Egyptians knew it as the craft of the vulture—a symbol of the astute effectiveness of the royal nature.

It's the grand strategist alone who recognizes the approach of such moments of opportunity. It's this perspective that grants the Sovereign an overview of the terrain, that shows when, strategically speaking, the battle is already won. Properly prepared, it's the opportunist who can seize these emerging moments of opportunity because they know what they're looking for, and how present conditions might fit into an overall plan.

CHALLENGE:

Attaining a Meta-Vision

Basic Concept: The wholeness of your mission as a Grand Vision. The Meta-Vision is the activation of a mind-state congruent with the needs of your overall plan.

Image: The great Eye hovering in a triangle above a truncated pyramid.

Challenge: Develop a higher (meta) vision that is expansive and far-thinking. Disregard perspectives locked in perpetual blindness of circumstance and reaction. Train yourself in the art of snatching victory from defeat.

Action: Begin the practice of mentally rising above a situation while keeping your grand vision in mind. Develop the skill of seeing through the hawk's eye, a perspective unencumbered by the entanglements of the present moment. Use this perspective to understand conditions as they are forming, to foresee difficulties and to strategize for success.

A Bit of Science

If strategy could be considered a science, then it represents the best skill to develop during this challenge. While strategy suggests having a grand vision and overall plan, it also admits that things seldom turn out as predicted. The best that we can do is adapt our strategies as conditions change, becoming as flexible as the proverbial bamboo reed. While strategic thought can and should be studied, strategies are rarely cut-and-dried formulas for success. Instead, they hint at a way of looking at the world, one attuned to moments of opportunity that open and close with each move on the chessboard of life.

Having a grand vision makes a person conscious of specific opportunities to look for and certain dangers to avoid. Attaining a meta-vision allows the Individual to rise above the chaos of the battlefield and achieve an overview of the terrain. From here they can be alert to moments when opportunities arise and develop strategies for maximizing present circumstances to leverage future advantages.

Napoleon was a master strategist. He rose from obscurity to become Emperor of Europe in a very short time. He masterfully engineered reversals of fortune, a key strategic skill, and an essential element of opportunism. Many of his victories were wrestled from moments that seemed to imply his defeat. But it was in these exact moments that his overview of the situation allowed him to claim victories to which others were blind because their limited perspectives were stuck in the dirt, chaos, and bloodshed of the battlefield. Napoleon himself said that battles were grand illusions. His success was born from an ability to see past those illusions and command a direct apprehension of forming situations. This talent gave him the ability to seize opportunities as they manifested out of changing events.

Something Mystical

There is a reason why Horus, the God of Kingship, is a hawk. Flying high above the terrain, hawks have a commanding overview of the situation. They hover above their hunting ground, and at the right moment, they swoop down and claim their prey.

Like the vulture, the hawk wastes no energy.

The vulture is well known for its opportunistic prowess. It waits until the work is done, then it feasts. Why waste valuable energy pecking at a meal that still has the energy to fight back? Instead, the vulture has the perspective to see what is ineviable for limping prey, and the patience to wait for its proper fruition. Like the hawk, a farsighted vision is a key to ruthless efficiency.

My Experience

Repeatedly throughout life, I watched as what seemed like a good situation degenerated into a thicket of brambles and then was awestruck to find what seemed like a terrible situation yield some jewel that I had not anticipated. Over and over again I found myself elated by events that later let me down and angered by events that eventually worked out to my benefit. The problem was that my perspective was stuck at ground level and only able to perceive (and respond to) what seemed to be immediately happening.

This happened so often that, once I caught on to the pattern, I began the habit of being skeptical when things appeared to be going well and looking for the hidden opportunities when my five senses said that things were surely doomed. I wanted to develop this skill to salvage my perspective whenever I felt carried away by strong emotions generated by hope and fear.

Rather than succumbing to the distress of immediate obstacles or panicking at the approach of moments that seemed barren of hope, having a Grand Vision allows a person to consider (and lay the framework for) far-reaching strategies and potential opportunities forming in the dawns of days yet to come.

LAPIS EXILIS

INITIATION

CHAPTER EIGHT

Contact Your Inner Initiator

"The Holy Guardian Angel is the spiritual
Sun of the Soul of the Adept."

-Aleister Crowley

There's an antiquated document written by a man named Abramelin to his son Lacmesh. In its pages, he describes for his son a magical ritual whose successful completion would result in the ability to contact and communicate with the Individual's "Holy Guardian Angel." It suggested that from this connection would come blessings in the form of certain gifts, powers, insights, and creative abilities.

In the literature of mysticism, this concept carries a great deal of mythological weight. The gift of raw, original creativity is powerful precisely because the authenticity of its signature cannot be forged with any quality. Counterfeit genius is like lightning in a bottle.

Communion with this mythical source refers to an electrical connection whose current is the substance of genius. Within the creative products of this genius, lives the spirit of their father, the mysterious creator-god who seeds the world with the ideas of all that might become.

The Living Presence of the Creative Self is the King's Zen.

The Individual who masters the dynamic harmony between the conscious and unconscious elements at work within themselves can gain access to powerful creative gifts. However, the true nature of these gifts is presently unexplainable.

Throughout history, certain Individuals have left compelling evidence of having tapped into profound and almost otherworldly (might we say divine?) states of creative consciousness. Those who achieve access to these states often use them to move the world in a way both astonishing and unpredictable. It is these Sovereign Individuals who typically are responsible for inaugurating changes in the generation to which they are born. Their lives represent the living presence of the creative self within.

It's the life of this type of Individual who brings forth an awareness and an awakening of irrevocably relevant knowledge, previously hidden. This often reveals itself by the mysterious but unmistakable synchronicity of their actions with greater cosmic laws eminently relating to present circumstances.

To know oneself at this level is to know, in the fullness of heart, what one must be doing and to what "end" one's life must naturally and willfully tend. Excuses cannot prevail here because the Individual has recognized in their True Will the existence of their very own "living must."

The activation of this type of deep awareness is like a lightning strike whose life is but its own and whose power manifests as something undeniable. It's this "lighting within consciousness" whose channeled force embodies a mystical authority beyond dispute. By its very nature, it proves itself to be beyond containment and unbound by the limitations of reason. It shocks the dull with its flashes of insight and alarms the commonplace with abilities sharply in contrast to their own preconceived limitations.

The Kingdom is: The Individual's expanding realm of Genius.

Knowing this force is to become it, and to become a force of Nature.

What connects a person to this force is the Inner Initiator—that inner part of one's being who speaks wisdom, who is wise, and whose sole objective is to Initiate the Individual in the curriculum of inner wisdom. It's the Inner Initiator that will, as a hidden source of guidance, unleash the embedded wisdom and inherent genius of one's very own psyche.

This transpersonal guidance activates a transformation capable of leading to unprecedented levels of personal awareness, growth, and evolutionary power. It's subtle because it is so mutable, but powerful beyond measure when compared with the effort-to-product ratio of the rational efforts of reasoned creations.

Develop a deep passion,
to serve one's own Living Muse,
as the force of the Creative Self,
and give it a life within life,
through creation's process-
an artfully inspired
willfully created,
expression
of the
Self.

Keeping this connection requires the Individual to bring an end to the mind's interference and its intervening noise. A period of quietude from days to months will assist the process. The length of time required is simply the length of time it takes to become aware (within one's consciousness) of the Inner Initiator's "magnetized" element.

This element makes itself know in certain unique ways, with clues that can be connected. Like a detective discerning the motive of the culprit from the kind of shoes he was wearing, the Individual must take up the examination of the contents of their mind in a similar way. The gold-of-Self must be sifted and collected from the contents of one's psychological structure. The Inner Initiator's movements and migration patterns can be elicited from certain subtle flashes of insight. In this way the Individual tracks the prey, drawing out the deeper meanings hidden both within and behind the contents of their inner workings.

So often it is the contents of the mind, that babbling surface structure, that is camouflaging the Inner Initiator's deep subconscious wisdom. When properly invoked, this subconscious spirit can manifest things through the Individual that may boggle the mind. In mysterious ways, it demonstrates that it is in itself force to be reckoned with. It's through subtle cryptic messages, composing themselves in consciousness that the Inner Initiator communicates across the distance of unconscious awareness.

It is through Self-Mastery that the Kingdom can be Ruled

The voice of the Inner Initiator calls for the consciousness of the Individual to become a student to its teachings. In ways both direct and subtle, painful and dramatic, the Inner Initiator teaches with a corrective rod in one hand and a rewarding apple in the other.

Messages begin coming through as inspirations and illustrations sketched in hieroglyphic moments. Sequences of informative consciousness arise layered, compounded, and with a unity of their own. Revelations bloom with an overall structure that conceives itself whole, from out of the void. From one's very own being, a work of art is born, already completed at its conception. From out of the mind's dark womb, new things emerge.

In the writings of the Inner Initiator, and even more in the shadows of these writings, emerge sacred texts with transcendental meanings expressed with elaborate and intelligent orchestration. These hieroglyphic messages build upon themselves block by block, words as bricks, all attending the summit of a great pyramid.

In silence, the King meditates, awaiting the next sublime scribbling to reveal itself and its teaching. In this state of consciousness, ample wisdom and insight come forth in a strange and unusual language, illuminated like signals disguised as everyday events.

The Individual may only understand a part of what that exotic mind is communicating, but nevertheless they must interpret it and give it a meaning that has a real use, and develop a method of understanding it that gives these intimate messages from the Self a foundation of real-life application—allowing these insights a chance to serve as utilities of one's being, as powers at hand for making one's way in the world.

Increasing Mastery of Domain

Stories still circulate of Individuals, "thousands of years ago," who managed to habitually operate in congruence with their Higher Self during their lifetime. Today these legends are still known and talked about as if they represent the only river that ever flowed pure and fresh.

Mastery, rituals, magic, and the power of the unconscious Self are looked upon superficially as fantastic daydreams, enchanted fables, and technologically disproven realities of faraway places and imagined falsehoods called "the entire ancient world."

Mostly, if we wanted to ignore the formative bulk of human civilization, we could. It only requires that we ignore it by dismissing the products and teachings of the millions of minds and millions of lives that composed the world's most mighty civilizations.

But... then there are the monuments, and all the works of art whose structure and composition baffles. It is these mysterious monuments whose precision put us in awe and whose methods imply unexplainable demonstrations of mastery. They prompt us to consider the possibility of the existence of some power unknown or suppressed until now. What this means really cannot be said.

What was the source of the powers that once caused civilizations to flourish? The Gods? Symbolic masters of all those fairy tales resigned to occult magic?

It's a subject difficult to accurately articulate in post-modern language because its language is spoken only by one's Inner Initiator, a dialect formed of an immaterial, language of consciousness. To make it even more difficult, it requires the knowledge of everything from the Earth to the Stars. That's a lot of talking.

Simply put, the Gods are composed of internal experience created neurologically. The source of that experience is one's very own neurological Tree of Life. It's the Individual's neurological Tree of Life that grows with initiation. It has been rooting and branching with each successive phase that the Initiate completes.

Initiation proceeds each phase of growth, an initiation into new circumstances that consequently encourages the mind to root ever deeper into the unconscious. As the roots of self-understanding grow deeper, the branches of self-expression naturally grow higher. At each phase the neurological tree expands its reach, multiplying its potential points for setting blossoms. It is these symbolic blossoms, as personal potentials, whose careful tending might yield a treasure yet unfathomed.

As Sovereign Individuals, what we do must be rooted deeply within ourselves, to the point where all action finds its ultimate root to be firmly secured in the heart of our own being. It's by the light of this internal oracle, the Inner Initiator, that the King advances into the unknown with a self-made torch.

The Oath of the King is an Ultimate Responsibility for the Kingdom.

The role of the King implies stewardship and tending. A King lives by the law of True Will and yet, by tending the Kingdom, is "doing work that is bigger than himself" at the same time.

As each task presents itself the King must ask, "Will this action keep me congruent with my values and Grand Vision?" This is the question that rules the Kingdom.

A King is an Individual who is saying to themselves: "Everything I do is about and for: _____

_____."

(And they know beyond doubt what fills in the rest of that statement.)

A King looks upon the tending of the affairs of the Kingdom as a great devotional work whose primary objective is for the Individual to "own who they are," as they are the Kingdom.

To "own oneself" means having the capacity to create and maintain a mind-state in harmony with one's Grand Vision. The whole journey, including every challenge and initiation, leads upward to the experience of mastery, to the attainment of a sovereign mind-state. It's in the experience of this "state" that the rewards of mastery begin blooming.

Mastery is the ability to manufacture flow.

Mastery teaches a person to bring their full presence to the moment and bring pure focus on that which they "absolutely know" they want.

This allows them to behave in a self-assured way. It allows them to consider matters and act with precise and instantaneous decisiveness. As a willful, purpose-driven Individual they can narrow their focus on their objective as if bearing down on a target from above.

To bring all of one's focus on a thing is to exchange extensiveness for intensiveness.

In this way, it's possible to magnify control over one's consciousness, and by proxy, one's kingdom.

As time passes, incremental growth builds the master's pyramid. As the years pass, the committed Sovereign finds its aspiring structure has fewer and fewer equals.

The masterful life is lived in the presence of mystery. This mystery represents the personal fulfillment of destiny and the continual experience of the womb/tomb of transformation. The mightiest experiences in human consciousness are born of mystery, from a connection with the infinite. From this infinite mystery, the True Will is born, as are its artistically driven manifestations.

When, as destiny prescribes, the True Will does emerge, some will call it a demon, some will call it an angel, and some will call it genius.

Like Russian dolls emerging one from within the other, the True Will becomes ever more purified and subtle, constantly revealing more of its true essence. Deeper and deeper into the folds of consciousness the Sovereign goes—all the way down to the most concentrated substance of their divinely unique and perfumed being. It's in this alchemy of personal essence that the True Will, as the Individual's divine name, is revealed.

This divine name is a word of power. Kept as a sublime secret, it's the key to the Individual's world. With this word, granted by the Inner Initiator, the Sovereign may now walk with confidence into the unknown.

CHALLENGE:

Application for Initiation

Contact Your Inner Initiator

Basic Concept: The Individual possesses a subconscious intelligence that acts as the living presence of the Creative Self and is the Individual's own internal source of authority and guidance. The Inner Initiator connects the Individual with their higher faculties and acts as the mediator between the Individual and the Gods, God, Universe, Source, etc.

Image: Hexagon

Challenge: Become attuned to the transpersonal guidance of the Inner Initiator. Work to consistently actualize a mind-state that is congruent with your Grand Vision.

Actions: Maintain internal congruence while becoming conscious of the subtle force of unconscious wisdom available to you from within. Practice the art of self-hypnosis if needed, to develop the proper state for becoming attuned to the resources available through the unconscious mind.

A Bit of Science

The practice of hypnosis is predicated on the understanding that our unconscious minds are a source of tremendous power and hidden resources. These become available to the Individual who knows the proper language for communicating with the unconscious mind and learns how to receive and transcribe its messages. The unconscious mind demonstrably possesses powers of which most people are only dimly aware. The ability of the unconscious mind to retain memories long lost to the conscious mind, or to be able to render pain inert, or to either form or transform the Individual's conscious representation of the world and overcome all sorts of difficulties forms the basis of hypnotherapy.

Developing this rapport with the unconscious mind also forms the basis of occult science. For our purposes of contacting the Inner Initiator, we might consider a seamless blend of the two, mixing trance states with various rituals that speak our intention to the unconscious mind in a language it understands. The transpersonal guidance of the Inner Initiator develops as a result of effectively cultivating a deep internal congruence between the conscious and unconscious minds.

Something Mystical

The true purpose of prayer, meditation, and ritual are to contact and commune with the Inner Initiator, although through the ages people have referred to this differently. It may come as little surprise to the Initiate at this point that what they have been cultivating is a connection with what might otherwise be called the "Inner God."

Depending on personal preference, it's been called many things, but it only takes a very few experiences with synchronicity to show the Individual that the Inner Initiator possesses mysterious powers and manifests its wisdom and guidance in unexplainable ways.

While it is generally recommended to keep one's commandments from and conclusions about the Inner Initiator a secret, one thing that can be said is that with increased contact its existence can come to be a profound and continuous influence in the Individual's life. Once awakened, its manifestations become more and more difficult to explain by any other than a symbolic, mystical language.

My Experience

From an early age, I had premonitions about the Inner Initiator. At times I experienced its overt influence as something mysterious and challenging to grasp. Through the achievement of certain "states," I was able to catch glimpses of its formative essence. When those "states" passed I was left with only a faint remembrance of its details.

Most of its influences seemed alien to me until I began an earnest study of the runes, shamanism, occultism, and mythology. I noticed that when I tried to discuss it most people showed a mixed response, seeming both uncomfortable and intrigued by the language of those systems. Later when I became a hypnotherapist, I found that the jargon of hypnosis and NLP allowed virtually the same things to be discussed in a way that certain people were more apt to grasp. Finding elements of truth in all these systems I chose to just synthesize them into what I now call "The Mind-State Arts."

After years of stop-and-go revelations, I decided to employ the strategy (and ritual) of that ancient text whose alleged origins were previously discussed. The text, known as *The Sacred Magic of Abramelin the Mage* is an occult classic, which outlines a process whereby an individual can make contact with their "Holy Guardian Angel" aka "The Inner Initiator."

Having possessed the book for over a decade and having read through it many times I was already familiar with the basics of the operation. The difficulty was the requirements: a residence in a secluded location, a room that could be dedicated as a temple, six months of near-complete seclusion during which the operator was allowed to do no servile work of any kind and was to dedicate their time to various ritual practices, purifications, and meditations with ever-increasing intensity for the duration of the six moons.

The complexities and involvement of the ritual are far more than this short section could allow, but needless to say, they require the full participation of every faculty of the operator for months on end, which in turn requires every ounce of will from the operator to complete. After the six moons, the operation is finally concluded with a very intense and dramatic (many would say terrifying) ritual in which the Individual's Holy Guardian Angel visibly appears and grants a specific (and essential) piece of knowledge. From the conclusion of the ritual onward, the Individual possesses the experience of a profound inner truth and has opened the channel to freely receive communications from this higher source who resides eternally within them.

After ten years of being familiar with this involved rite, a situation finally manifested in which all the requirements were available to carry the operation through to completion. Six months later I had documented a wealth of awe-inspiring, jaw-dropping revelations. It was the most extensive pursuit I had ever taken of that sort. One of its products is the book you now hold.

THE CALL

INITIATION

CHAPTER NINE

"The Unknown Self"
Accepting the Unfathomed Possibilities That
Still Lie Ahead

"...only one who has risked the fight with the dragon and is
not overcome by it wins the hoard, the 'treasure hard to attain.'
He alone has a genuine claim to self-confidence, for he has
faced the dark ground of his self and thereby has gained
himself. This experience gives some faith and trust...in the
ability of the self to sustain him, for everything that menaced
him from inside he has made his own. He has acquired the
right to believe that he will be able to overcome all future
threats by the same means. He has arrived at an inner
certainty which makes him capable of self-reliance."

-Carl Jung, The Symbolic Life

<u>The Reality</u>: things never imagined possible eventually come to pass.

Mastery requires, in the end, an all-encompassing openness to experience. Paradoxical because it requires both a binding focus to bring about the culmination of a completed level of purpose, and also a complete release; the act of letting go and moving beyond it.

Every child does this in infancy, born into this world and, consequently, leaving the womb behind. The womb forms us and brings us into being, then we go through successive stages that mark birth, life, and death.

Like initiation itself, there is a beginning, middle, and end of all things.

Knowing where one is at in this process helps to determine whether winter is coming, and our work is only cultivating dead conditions or whether spring is here and it's time to plant seeds in fertile ground.

When the child moves beyond the womb or the chicken breaks free from its egg, they each have completed a level of purpose. A completion is also an act of destruction. It is the destruction of previous circumstances.

Birth implies outgrowing something, and a death that seems so apparent is actually a broken world that's been outgrown. It would have become a prison to your development had you not broken free.

Eggs and wombs are comfortable places. They're hard to leave willingly. To break out of comfort, even when it's becoming cramped, is to break into a New World. That's one of the many mythological lessons of the Gnostic god Abraxas.

At the same time that an Individual is breaking out of old but familiar conditions, unpredictability is breaking in—into their consciousness.

What is new is unfamiliar. Evolution produces something new.

The further we travel upon our evolutionary path the more likely we are to begin encountering things that we could not have foreseen.

Situations and circumstances that we could never have imagined may emerge either as fortune by which we shall profit or conversely as unknown debts of Karma desiring collection—those old romances who still possess a little sting!

In this World, a new awareness may emerge at any moment. The Unknown Self may emerge at any time and unexpectedly begin expanding toward a totally new and previously unknown horizon.

The universe is infinite, and all accomplishments are relative. Mastery is the steppingstone for greater mastery. The path travels on. Once a baby masters crawling, they begin walking as a rookie. When we graduate high school as a senior, we begin college as a freshman.

Mastery. Completion. Success. Fulfillment. But! Only of another phase of a vast train of uncountable phases of being.

Each life is one more skin shed. Each success is the completion of one more block in the two and a half million that is the construction of the great pyramid of experience. Completion of existence means the fulfillment of all experiences of all kinds, and their synthesis into a new form of universal understanding.

The Sovereign, having completed this awesome task of consciousness, may at last lay down their pen and brush and set aside the tools of their completed work. They may now feast upon that which lies beyond the crimson curtains. They may, at last, relinquish the pains of body and the anguish of mind that preceded that honeymoon of spirit.

Finally freed to enjoy that which is most desired, the Sovereign undresses from their creation and removes the last garments that compose their very conception of a limited Self.

Now naked of all traces of earlier limitations, they may secure that pearl of great price, that which is the fulfillment of endless longing. With nothing more to accomplish they realize the ultimate value of the journey itself, and its ordeals. The path has indeed become the goal and realizing this, the resurrecting spirit turns once again to renew that longing by moving back into the dark folds of a new creation.

The ultimate sum of all learning is the End.

All learning leads to the end because it sets in motion a process of inevitability. The Individual will learn, the Individual will grow. This growth will gain momentum, and in time, whether great or small, that Individual will at last, come to conclusions.

It is these conclusions that the Individual must resolve, extracting the essential essences of their meanings.

What is of essential value becomes part of the treasury. Nothing less than brass is even considered.

Our experiences cannot be empty. Things must add up to something.

Even unpleasantness must be mined for its value. Every experience must give something to the Individual. They must exact the tax.

Whatever happens, the Sovereign Individual must find a way to turn it into an event of value. Becoming an opportunist, they must embrace the potential that exists in moments of chaos, confusion, change, decay, and uncertainty.

Why would confusion and chaos greet the master after all this hard work?

The truth? The truth is those moments of darkness greet one and all alike, but while many choose to run from this fact, the master is the one who is moving to greet it, by cultivating an opportunistic approach to its emerging presence in the ever-changing biosphere of life.

Conditions can never stay the same, which is why an Individual can master their conditions and yet in time still fall from that grace. There are no static positions or static situations. The Earth is spinning round and round on its axis, and the World and all its contents are moving with it. Change is incessant. It's a bad world for concrete. It's doomed to crack. It is inevitable that the sidewalk will have to be re-poured.

The Facts:

No matter how strong one's position is

No matter how extensive one's wealth is

No matter how powerful current defenses seem

No matter how much one tries to preserve the conditions of forms—conditions change and so do forms.

Life is dynamic, there are no static positions.

The Sovereign Individual must remain eternally prepared to abandon conditions that no longer inspire vitality. At the same time, the Individual must remain open to actively receiving new awareness with courage.

To fear and dread the experience of "rupture" is an archetypal fear of primal origin imprinted in the collective unconscious. It's a universal dread. Its archetypal experience is what the Tower card of the tarot deck attempts to capture. It's an initiatory experience, the destruction of cherished knowledge, the end of a particular model of the World. On the card, lightning is depicted striking a tower, fracturing it, setting it to flame, with bodies falling from its unforgiving heights.

This is the image of initiated change. It's the experience of that moment when one realizes both the tragedy and the freedom contained in strikes of lighting. It's that appalling flash that signals "the tower's coming down."

It's one of the most dramatic events consciousness can experience. It is, like death itself, a signal to the conscious mind that the end of an era is here. The old order no longer stands. There's a new sheriff in town and he ain't abidin' by the old way.

This is life, over and over and over again. It has been played out in a million different scenarios in a similar way. It's a cycle, a journey that completes itself in time. Things are created, and then things are destroyed. There's no way of stopping the process.

We must develop internal stability. Yet the skills we develop to do this must take into account the instability of the external world.

Learning to opportunistically adapt to changing circumstances means we must develop skills that have the power to meet both the realized demands and the potential demands of life.

This means remaining fluid and adaptable so that the chaos of the battlefield of life can be made into a blessing when others see only the curse. It means that conditions that would crush the commonplace person are the same conditions that empower the Sovereign Individual.

It's by teaching ourselves to be acutely aware of the changing demands of the moment that we become masters of emerging possibilities. It's this exercise in flexible opportunism that strategically shifts its weight as doors open and close with each additional move on the chessboard of life. It's through the strategy of indefatigable ingenuity that we make the most of every change and transformation of conditions.

Like chess, every move changes the power dynamics of the board.

Situations shift until they hold almost no resemblance to what they once were. The bottoms of oceans are pushed to the tops of the mountains. Life transforms through cycles of initiation.

Mastery is the "actualization"—the real results of all that was longed for from a specific phase of life.

Everything that has seemed to happen externally has really been just a prop of consciousness, to cause it to evolve. The process goes on and on. There's no end to rush to. There's no reward for which you can't wait. There is no day when it will be done. Now is as good as ever: to begin, to end, to move forward in conquest, to upgrade through sacrifice, to experience life in a new way, to discover something unknown about yourself, to perform the ritual of your own becoming, to actualize your deepest desires, to move into the unknown with fearlessness.

When we know, then we're done.

To be open requires that we look at the World in a new way, occasionally abandoning our learning, and our wisdom, and the things we are certain of and put them down so that we can be like children again who know nothing, and who know that they know nothing and are open to learning. In this open state, they are far more attentive than any adult and learning at a much faster pace. The child who knows little or nothing is in a far better position to be educated than an adult with a Ph.D.

What an Individual doesn't know will find them, and they had best be ready to receive it when it does. This is important because becoming a Sovereign Individual is a process of making oneself unbreakable and moving beyond the possibility of defeat by developing an attitude and disposition that is capable of elastic strategy.

The King cannot foresee everything. Those things that can be seen, that do lie ahead should be noted, precautions taken, and plans made, as they are possible.

But no strategy is absolute, no position is "the position," no one is "the one." No condition is the only condition, and conditions will always change. We must be able to change to meet those conditions in the most opportunistic manner possible.

Change is a break in the structures of power. A break in its structure is a release of its power, and hence power is available to direct in any moment of change.

As a Sovereign Individual, the natural processes of your unconscious mind will pull you, as if by an internal gravity, towards the gate of initiation, to the ending and beginning of a phase, and onward in a journey in which you are the evolving substance. You are becoming the elixir of the alchemical gold, you are cultivating the neurological Tree of Life within, you are setting in motion a ritual that is leading to a point where you are the absolute Sovereign of yourself, your being, and your destiny. The power and the method to do this is in your hands now.

CHALLENGE:

Application for Initiation

The Unknown Self

Accepting the Unfathomed possibility that still lies ahead

Basic Concept: Life is a process evolving through a series of states, each development completing a level of purpose and ultimately yielding something unexpected or unanticipated. What was hoped for at the beginning of the journey (hopes formed of inexperience) is different than the reality that exists at the end of the journey (awareness now informed by experience).

Image: The Stars of the Infinite night sky, the Egyptian Goddess Nuit

Challenge: Develop your sense of destiny, mystery, and mastery of transformation. Embrace the fact that the successful fulfillment of another phase of being means moving beyond that completion and back into the dark folds of a new creation.

Action: Learn to recognize stages of completion so that you may reappraise and modify your strategy and ultimate objective.

A Bit of Science

In the exploration of space and the outer cosmos, every new step and every new discovery holds the potential to bring to light some unknown fact that could require the revaluation of all former "knowledge." It was Nietzsche who famously suggested a reevaluation of all values when he foresaw the changes emanate in the development of the modern world. Similarly, we now live at the end of the postmodern era and a reevaluation is once again in order. Daily it seems that another thing which we deemed certain and definitive is being resigned to the class of discredited or debunked knowledge.

The farther one goes through space or time the more likely one will be required to reevaluate their assumptions.

Something Mystical

Mysticism is an experience of unknown possibilities. Many have suggested that the very idea of God is an idea of the Unknown Self. This level of initiation is the very definition of "something mystical."

My Experience

The longer I live, the more I change. The more I come to know myself, the more the Unknown Self makes its presence known. The more experiences I have, the more I am in awe of the unfathomed possibilities that still lie ahead.

EPILOGUE

Conceiving SELF in an Immortal Medium

What to say about the eventual end of everything?

How shall the Sovereign individual go about the business of establishing their divine Will in the World in spite of mortality?

What will be the necessary strategy for overcoming the blows to wisdom received by the wise at every step along the way?

The Epilogue, like a eulogy, is by its nature a testament to the inevitable. It is a baffled, self-reconciliation whose humility is constructed of confounded human bewilderment—an utterly natural expression in the face of an experience associated with a confrontation with the Infinite.

This is the eulogy of Kingship. It's the transition from the active phases of mortal human life to the omnipotence whose circumference is the end of existence. Here the enemy of Osiris waits, poised for battle. It is because of the malice of this enemy that Osiris must spring to life again and again. Myth credits Isis, goddess of Nature, for arousing the King Osiris back to life.

As the myth reveals, the capacity to overcome death is a function of Nature herself. As formidable as death may seem, it should be noted that the bulk of human religion and spiritual practice has been created to reassure the Individual that yes, they do indeed possess the capacity and the potential to surpass its limits.

The purpose of every item in the Pharaoh's tomb, the contents of each hidden chamber and its treasure, every amulet, and every spell writ upon the walls—was an attempt to prepare the consciousness of the King to overcome the chaotic dissolution of death and enter into the realm of infinity.

The symbol for this experience of infinity was the goddess of the unveiled stars of the night sky, Nuit. Imagined almost in the context of a seductive mistress, she invites the worshiper into her. Her robe is covered in stars like that of the night sky. Sweetly, she desires nothing more than "the wholehearted rapture of ecstasy" in the experience of her.

To this most divine end of consciousness, the King seeks, at last, to ultimately fulfill his desire. It's to this end, in the eternal, that our consciousness does tend. There is no greater desired intimacy possible than the desire to enter into this exotic mistress. Even now, she is within your neurological tree, invisible in her envelopment.

To get a glimpse of her (infinity)—one would either need to be outside of the Universe itself completely, looking in, or undergo this process, this ritual initiation, this love affair with entering her, again and again until the sum of your being becomes equal to hers.

This is the ultimate desire: TO BECOME EQUAL WITH THE ALL.
...to slip into her infinite folds, and experience the silk knowledge of her boundless circle, to be granted access to that place beyond constraint.

It's the passion for this embrace that drives consciousness. It is the not-so-secret agenda of libido and hence, the motive of all activities—earthly or celestial.

Now enters the Hero to claim this prize. The Individual has become Hero, and the Hero has become a King. Through "becoming" consciousness has proven its worth, its strength, its might, and the integrity of its lust for life.

It has shown its value as a lover, and so Man-become-Master takes his seat at the feast, he pulls himself up to the table where the infinite offers herself. He's made himself a perfect sacrifice of WILL—finally, his consciousness is ready for its great reward and the even greater adventure prepared ahead.

"The sea that calls all things unto her calls me,
and I must embark. For, to stay, is to freeze and
crystallize and be bound in a mould."

-Kahil Gibran

The Initiate has become a consciousness who is both prepared and willing to give ALL ...and so becomes worthy to "rend her veil."

This symbolic storyline reflects the most seductive of all the seductresses—the model herself for all seduction and those who practice its art. In the spiritual tradition from which her myth originates in ancient Egypt, she is the boundless night sky. She represents infinity, and she also "swallows the Sun," symbolically the King, at the end of each day.

Through her body, the Sun King travels—through the infinity of being—until inevitably birthed from her again as the dawn of a New Sun on the rise again, and again, and again.

This experience of Infinity is the symbolic breaking, once again, of the chick through the egg.

Yet, this EGG is much bigger than anything else in the Universe because it is the Universe. This bird bursting through is like the phoenix-of-the-all. This egg is itself the Individual's universe, and what lies beyond possesses the power to swallow their consciousness whole and absorb its substance entirely, as the grain of sand it has become.

The physical form of the finite and mortal self must someday meet the Unknown Self that lies beyond. As a physical object amongst time and space, the body is committed to dissolving along with all its efforts—unless!—precautions are taken: that of securing action designed to transmute its form into an immortal medium.

The imprint of the Sovereign's True Will must impregnate an enduring substance, one chosen for legacy. A King's Will must cast its seed into a fertile place beyond the contact or influence of the World that changes.

An enduring and monumental legacy is the primary artistic concern of all works of Kingship. It's the essence of things Kings build. The traditional medium for expressing the enduring Will of the Sovereign Individual has been monuments of immovable stone, precisely aligned with chosen stars.

Once aware of that particular cosmic force (star) with which one's heart is truly aligned, the work of immortalizing its testament in metaphoric stone may proceed. In this work one seeks to capture the essential essence of True Will itself: mysterious and baffling, perplexing and awe-inspiring, disturbingly divine and terrifying terrestrial. Ascending as an aspiration unencumbered by ordinary fetters, the pyramid of True Will is built in accord with a magical law in a terrain beyond the limits of reason.

There can become a sort of awe-induced doubt at the Eulogy. Its moment is the confrontation with certain knowledge. It's the showdown with suppressed knowledge. It manifests in a final gasp, and a final thought, which is the final realization!

That final realization: of the existence of forces possessing strength, power, and consciousness beyond any reasonable explanation.

Before the Individual's very eyes, the naked splendor of the volup-
tuous body of the goddess Nuit is revealed! In the ecstasy of her love, the
powers of infinity are flaunted. Into the overwhelming arms of a boundless embrace goes the drop of that finite personality into the ocean of an
impersonal love's infinite grace.

In a moment, the cloak of perceived limitation is lost, just a drop
consumed in the current of waves that crest upon an everlasting ocean
of ecstasy. Fueled by this eventuality, the Initiate knows that even their
individuality will one day be consumed by infinity. Thus, to impregnate
infinity with the fingerprint of individual Will is the ultimate magical
attainment. It's the Pharaonic mission, to connect one's consciousness
with the stars, and in that union, conceive an immortal destiny.

The most enduring physical structure is the pyramid. It's in this
shape that our efforts are modeled. To attain those piercing heights, all
must be secured in origins—bedrock. The structures we build to represent our Will must endure.

The base of a pyramid is in proportion to its summit. The math is
basically simple. Yet as the pyramid ascends, it does so to a point... it
ends in infinity. There its root connects with the Universe. Our Will
also must be firmly rooted, like the pyramid, immovable. Its base must
be solid in the world, a quaternary structure, four-sided and aligned
with the four directions and four seasons that mark the beginning and
end of all things. Simply said, our Will must incorporate the shape of
nature herself if it is to endure.

It's in the pyramid's shape, in the medium of eternity, that we must
metaphorically cast our signatures.

The myth of Osiris calls our attention both to the eternal and the
finite tendencies of life: to cycle, and to spring forth, again and again,
and again, enduring through a renewal of ever-evolving forms. Within
our unconscious mind there exists a collection of these embedded
images from past sagas of existence, carried in our blood and written
into our genetic code.

The potential to become a Sovereign Individual, and to follow the divine path of True Will to the soul's completion is the "Great Work" to which each consciousness is called. It is the voice of Nuit herself which calls us to that finality; to at last merge one's completed consciousness with the universe herself, thus becoming as infinite as her boundless circle.

This is the divine destiny of Kings, to rise from Earth unto the Heavens. The strength of Will required to complete this journey can be activated via the genetic material contained in one's blood. It's by way of this precious gift in the blood, inherited from Kings of the past that we claim our Crown. It's the blood of these Kings, who cast their noble seed into every fertile field in the Kingdom, that we honor when we claim our Sovereignty.

Each Individual must look at themselves in the mirror for that mark—that stamping of the "primal father" whose vigor did cast its seed and set its mark upon all its future kin of consciousness.

It's this remarkable seed of unconscious knowledge, inherited from sacred origins, that contains the blueprint of our sovereign potential. It's this potential, manifest as one's genetic uniqueness, that is the fingerprint of one's unique consciousness. It's this fingerprint whose life shall echo across the ages. It's this Will-in-the-blood that "calls" the Individual to Sovereignty.

It is also this Will-to-become that casts the seeds of that becoming into the fertile womb of the great mistress herself. In this way the Sovereign Individual calls their Will to life, again and again, announcing from aeon to aeon, "I WILL ENDURE."

It is this "Will-to-endure" that evolves the Individual's consciousness through successive phases and incarnations until the ecstatic completion of the Great Work.

Consciously evolving means "strategic synthesis." A King reincarnates until all experience has been completed, until his conscious is equal to the All. Unto this end the sovereign consciousness continuously evolves, taking on new forms to meet the demands of new conditions.

These new conditions are upon us now.

Currently, they are requiring all who hear "the Call" to birth a new culture. This new culture of Sovereign Individuals must establish kingdoms of their own, ruling from within; kingdoms whose substance possesses the tenacity to endure the convergence of life's conflicting powers and is capable of negotiating a reconciliation of life's opposites through the synthesis of complementary arrangements.

This is just a description of what an expert mason might call "solid building." Establishing a base for this Kingdom may seem to involve an exhaustive preparation. Merely clearing away and preparing a place from which to work may absorb a great deal of one's efforts.

But with the completion of that immense preparation—getting the "cornerstone" of one's Grand Vision aligned, level, and plumb—the project can then begin to progress steadily upward toward ultimate completion.

Establish your base—that is the bulk of the work, and most of the heavy lifting.

All else is built upon that stone and from that foundation. Alignment is the only enduring concern.

Nothing more need to be measured. Block by block the pyramid rises. As the rhythm of its construction is mastered, the work continues developing on its own, almost unconsciously the pyramid rises, surpassing the efforts of conscious thought.

Aligned with Nature, it has the momentum of Nature on its side. Like the Nile's eternal waters, so flows the Individual's own current of Will—and as the Nile, it shall continue unto the Great Sea and into infinite and unformed worlds yet to be.

This book tells of the existence of an eternal heritage, which is in the blood and bones of the Individual's being. It evokes a story written in the Individual's genetic consciousness. At its magnum opus, the Individual's unique story is discovered to be a story shared, and as timeless as consciousness itself. Not alone, but in the company of prophets and heroes, pharaohs and kings, has the Individual been traveling.

The eternal Pharaoh still rules. A voice of wisdom emanates from the heart, and like Pharaoh that heart cannot be moved. The voice is from upon high. It gives "The Call" which is the first establishment of its reign. Its voice is from beyond, so mysterious and so wise. Yet one finds it's also one's own voice, addressing the godhood of one's own Self.

Through this initiation, the internal dialogue has been transformed from the commonplace drivel of fret and worry into inspiring words that lightening forth in symbolic life. In story and image, it proceeds as a fiery inner oratory that demonstrates the actualization of one's daemon. Now the muse of genius may burst forth as the living energy of the Higher Self.

As the Sun, as a King, as a lamp, as the light of consciousness, as the serpent of initiation, and in many other symbolic forms does the spirit of the Higher Self take for its sovereign form. The Individual who claims their Crown enters into a kingly brotherhood, a collegium of immortals who stand with torches in hand, welcoming the Initiate into a unique and archetypal reality—the Tao of Kings.

It's through the initiated efforts of this exalted company that the pillars of the pylon were first raised. It's these immortals of consciousness whose ancient and epic pursuits wrote their stories upon the eternal aether. Today their hieroglyphs can still be read, etched upon the fabric of dreams, and witnessed in the current of unconscious stirrings that inspire the mind and circulate in the blood.

The blood contains the key to the initiation of consciousness. Its circulation is the continuation of the journey of consciousness. It flows in currents through the body of the King—a force coming straight from the Heart. The path is within, and because of this, it is composed of materials within the Individual's own consciousness.

Simply put, your great ancestor was, in their own time and in their own way, where you are today at this very moment, and on the same path. With this Great Ancestor, you share your moments of doubt and exhilaration. With this Great Ancestor, you share the twists of fate that inevitably occur and recur throughout the course of natural life.

With this Great Ancestor, you share the consciousness of the hope and the despair, the ebb and flow, and the experience of light and dark that are unbound by time or culture.

Life is change, change, change, and to what end is all this change tending?

Toward home. Wherever that is, and whatever makes that real. The Egyptians oriented themselves to a home in the stars.

Whatever form your mystical home takes: whether the Garden of Eden, or the Garden of Wisdom, or Heaven, or Nirvana, or Valhalla, whatever it's called—it symbolizes Home.

"The Call" is the invitation for the Sovereign Individual to follow their path of True Will to its front doorstep. Making it home with one's Crown intact is all that really matters. One must not allow the world to break them. Instead, they must, in time, become the Master of their existence.

Like Odysseus, it's the aspiration to make it home that fortifies us through the trials and tribulations of life. It's upon this ancient path, and in flickering torchlight, that one can still see those faint outlines of hieroglyphic graffiti scribbled by ancestors who beheld these same archetypal challenges. It's in their footprints that we walk.

They are the footprints of those who succeeded, who survived, and who made it past the threshold of historic challenges TO LIVE ON. It's these great and immortal ancestors who cast their seeds of hope and desire into the womb of tomorrow's creation, and whose effects live on today echoing into the present, living on in our blood and bones.

The archetype of the King is a genetic seed of consciousness. This genetic consciousness is the living material of a reality that shall live on—in royal seeds cast forth by a generous hand into the fertile fields, which are the moments of today.

It's upon the walls of the subconscious mind's dimly lit corridors of initiation that shadowy messages dance across the threshold from these Great Ancestors.

Occasionally one can sense their presence, in the breath and being of forms that move like wisps of smoke, as a substance that drifts in and out of shape.

It's beyond these images that the Individual must eventually move as they transition from the finite to the infinite. The King shall one day become Emperor; trading a fleshy, finite, and unique expression of Self, for one that is transpersonal, infinite, and universal.

It's this strange energy that is behind even the Ancestor. It is undifferentiated. It has no form. To all conceivable comparisons, the energy behind it all and the form that has held it all together has in reality, held no reality—its reality is of the substance of absolutely nothing at all.

There is nothing we can experience that we have not also made up in our own mind.

In the entire Universe: nothing is forever.

How to deal with that? How to deal with the nothingness that's at the root of consciousness?

Its lesson is the journey of consciousness itself. It's our consciousness in the boat of the Sun-God Ra crossing the abyss of the night sky.

Change will come, and the question is and will always remain, what will be made of that change?

What will be fashioned from the combinations of the known and the unknown? What will emerge from the womb of one's own self-creation is of the essence of a great mystery.

When will it all end? It's a question that lingers on consciousness like a burden of despair.

How can we give of ourselves and seek great things when perpetually tailed by a ferocious and threatening shadow of almost constant uncertainty?

Why bother to suffer the threats certain in the adventures of seeking to further one's consciousness?

Answer: for one very good reason—it's not just the Hero who lives in the shadow of an eventual, inevitable physical demise. That is the fate of one-and-all; it is a fate sealed in time.

The difference lies in the choice of interpretations.

It's a choice which lies at the heart of the heroic life. By commanding the course of one's life and causing that life to take the shape of one's Will, a person moves away from mortal-minded fear and into a state of "immortalized becoming."

It's the Captain of the ship whose voyage, blessed, may be long, and being long the dangers encountered may be many, and being many the obstacles to be overcome may be of categories unknown.

We become this Captain, who commands the ship from port to port, from opportunity to opportunity, moving ever onward into our adventure of self-becoming. For knowledge and profit, we sail across the waves as Captain of Self and Spirit, upon the boat of consciousness, ever onward with the winds of True Will filling our sails and with unknown horizons beckoning.

Mysteriously those winds carry us forth upon the waters of life until the ship of one's consciousness is laden: with abundant gold, the priceless treasures of wisdom, and the luscious bounty of the love of women—and all of the good things imagined and made real by the King.

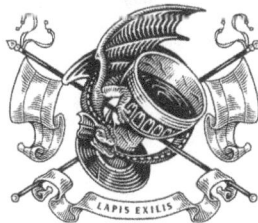

"The sea is dangerous and its storms terrible, but
these obstacles have never been sufficient reason to
remain ashore...Unlike the mediocre, intrepid spirits
seek victory over those things that seem impossible...
It is with an iron will that they embark on the most
daring of all endeavors...to meet the shadowy future
without fear and conquer the unknown."

-Attributed to Ferdinand Magellan

Spiritual Kingship is a path within.

This is a commitment to True Will,
a commitment to Oneself,
in the Absolute.

Admission to its gates is irrevocable.

Its gate was passed at one's birth into this World.

You passed the threshold long ago.

Now, at last, the Individual,
with eyes-wide-open,
and awe-dropped jaw:
recognizes
fully and deeply,
the awesome nature of the quest
that yet lies before consciousness,
and the unfathomable possibilities
that shall emerge
from the horizons of the Unknown
still forming in the dawns to come.

SUMMARY

An Overview of The King's Curriculum

The King's Curriculum is a unique system of spiritual self-development based on the art of Kingship. Its implications are vast, both for the individual who becomes a Sovereign and for the World which they call home.

Kingship is based on the practice of Self-Sovereignty, an elevated form of self-rulership. This self-rulership has some preliminary requirements. To rule oneself, one must first "know oneself." In this respect, the core teaching reflects the enlightened suggestion chiseled above the ancient oracle of Delphi—to Know Thyself.

In the act of coming to "know thyself" and establishing one's Sovereign consciousness, the Individual recognizes their "True Will" as their connection with the Universe, God, the Gods, Source, Higher Self, etc.

In a symbolic act, the Individual consummates the identification of their True Will with the Universal Will, uniting the two as one. Each is now seen as a reflection of the other.

Empowered by this figurative marriage, the Individual is free to live their True Will with the force of divine conviction, having come to understand the development of one's consciousness as essential to the development of universal consciousness.

This is the Crown of the Sovereign Individual: a realization both of the divinity inherent in one's True Will, and the activation of the power necessary to achieve it within the jurisdiction of its purpose. This becomes the Sovereign Individual's divine duty—to grant themselves the liberty to do their True Will, and nothing else.

In order to attain this identification with Universal Will, and to become its agent, the Sovereign Individual must disentangle themselves from "consensus trance"—that overt identification with the common current of humanity that is regulated by societal manipulation, that develops as a vagueness of personal conviction and that manifests as a sort of mass hypnosis.

In short, the act of hearing one's calling involves the blotting out of the background noise of society—its politics, its popularly held opinions, its suggestions, and its mutable system of ethics.

While this stance may seem revolutionary, its spirit is more accurately evolutionary. Its standpoint is less concerned with overthrowing mass consciousness and more concerned with establishing the Individual's evolutionary path based on the organic development of the Individual's own True Will.

It could be said that *The King's Curriculum* does not set itself to the task of solving "the world's" problems directly. Nor does it seek to offer solutions to the masses. Instead, it values and puts its emphasis on the unique perspective of the Individual's consciousness as becoming (like Buddha, Christ, and Odin) an independent force of evolution.

In this way problems are solved in the only way problems of consciousness can be solved—independently within the Individual's own consciousness. This method allows *The King's Curriculum* to achieve its objective, not by enforcing opinions and contrived beliefs for the sake of political gains, but instead by applying the evolutionary force of the Individual's consciousness upon the plane of consciousness, and in this way, to have an evolutionary effect upon its currents.

There is the well-known story of the monkeys on a particular island who began washing their food, and shortly thereafter the monkeys on a nearby island began doing the same although the two groups were "isolated." Similarly, the consciousness of the Sovereign Individual affects the universal currents of human consciousness.

The Sovereign Individual frees themselves, allowing themselves to live their True Will, which in turn, has the effect of assisting others to do the same through the ripples created by their pioneering consciousness. The path of the Spiritual King develops the key components of this attainment, namely the Crown, the Throne, and the Kingdom.

The Crown is the attainment of a state of consciousness in which the Individual realizes both their own True Will and the innate divinity of its calling.

The Throne is the Individual's power base. The True Will naturally calls the Individual to some attainment. The skills required to do this are embodied in the Throne. The Throne represents the development of the Individual's natural gifts and skills along with the development of those aspects of oneself required to both maintain one's state of Sovereignty and master the challenges required by one's values. In this way, the development of the Throne empowers and expands the influence of one's Will, furthering the fulfillment of one's authentic nature.

The Kingdom is the Individual's consciousness, their state of being, which is the medium through which they experience the world at large. The Kingdom also represents the connection to their duty as Sovereign, beginning with the governance of their state of being. The Kingdom is the place from which the Individual's ordering influence can begin to radiate outward into the external world, impregnating some medium with its spiritual imprint, reproducing itself in willed forms.

The Sovereign's duty is to their kingdom. The power to govern it is granted, and its jurisdiction determined, by the Individual's True Will and its stated purpose. As such, what falls outside of that purpose, no matter how important it may otherwise seem, must be regarded as being outside of one's jurisdiction of power. What is outside of one's realm may very well be within the jurisdiction of some other Sovereign being, in which case one must not act.

The Sovereign, in keeping to their stated purpose, their True Will, must exercise their powers within their jurisdiction, whose circle is the boundary of their Kingdom and whose borders define the extent of their duties as Sovereign. This symbolizes the effective realm of their power as defined by their own True Will. Once again, the Sovereign makes it a practice to do their True Will, and nothing else. Their influence is thus concentrated within their Kingdom. There is no leakage of its force by trying to control or manipulate foreign affairs.

The nine challenges that make up the Initiation into Spiritual Kingship are designed to strengthen the Individual's Will and calibrate one's moral compass, so it points to that true north which is symbolic of the Individual's True Will. The ultimate intention of this is to properly align the Individual with their calling, which is the source of their power. To this end, the Initiate develops their Will, and with it a sense of purpose. Once attuned to this force, the Individual trains themselves to maintain its direction through the many twists and turns of life. The ordeals common to attaining and maintaining this internal force are symbolically manifest in the nine challenges.

The intention of *The King's Curriculum*, its unique system of spiritual self-development, its initiation, and its curriculum, is to activate the potential already existing within the Individual's consciousness, to become a Sovereign being. This is achieved when the Individual is motivated to fulfill their life's purpose by manifesting its Grand Vision.

As the True Will manifests, it correspondingly develops the consciousness of the Individual. As it does, it contributes to the development of Universal Consciousness and thus plays its unwitting but divine part in the evolution of the World.

"There is always room for a Man of force, and he makes room for many."

-Ralph Waldo Emerson

THE MANIFESTATION OF SOVEREIGNTY

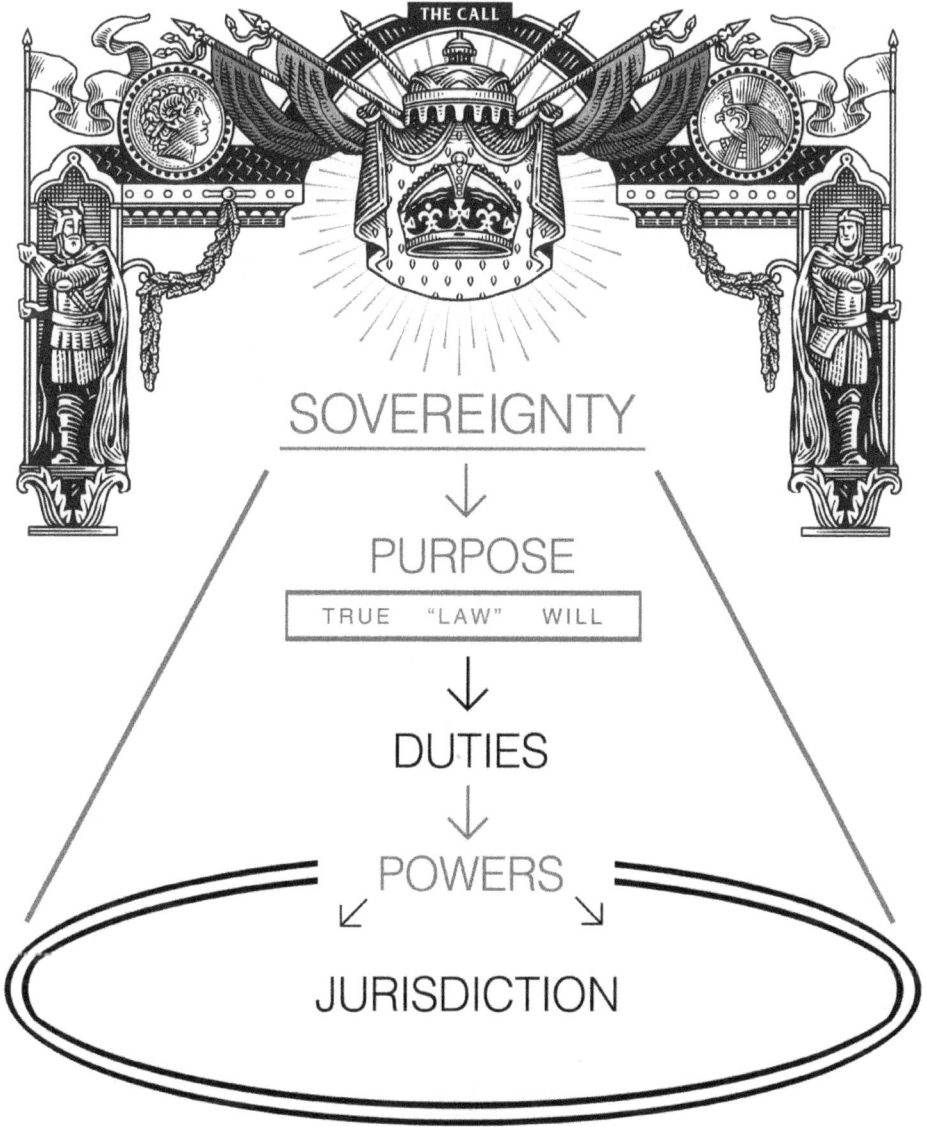

THE CALL

SOVEREIGNTY

↓

PURPOSE

TRUE "LAW" WILL

↓

DUTIES

↓

POWERS

JURISDICTION

THE CIRCLE

THE KINGDOM

LIVE YOUR WILL @ www.thekingscurriculum.com